NEW DIRECTIONS FOR COMMUNITY COLLEGES

Arthur M. Cohen
EDITOR-IN-CHIEF

Florence B. Brawer
ASSOCIATE EDITOR

A Practical Guide to Conducting Customized Work Force Training

Sherrie L. Kantor
Central Piedmont Community College

EDITOR

Number 85, Spring 1994

JOSSEY-BASS PUBLISHERS
San Francisco

Clearinghouse for Community Colleges

A PRACTICAL GUIDE TO CONDUCTING CUSTOMIZED WORK FORCE TRAINING
Sherrie L. Kantor (ed.)
New Directions for Community Colleges, no. 85
Volume XXII, number 1
Arthur M. Cohen, Editor-in-Chief
Florence B. Brawer, Associate Editor

LC 85-644753   ISSN 0194-3081   ISBN 0-7879-9957-1

NEW DIRECTIONS FOR COMMUNITY COLLEGES is part of The Jossey-Bass Higher and Adult Education Series and is published quarterly by Jossey-Bass Inc., Publishers, 350 Sansome Street, San Francisco, California 94104-1342 (publication number USPS 121-710) in association with the ERIC Clearinghouse for Community Colleges. Second-class postage paid at San Francisco, California, and at additional mailing offices. POST-MASTER: Send address changes to New Directions for Community Colleges, Jossey-Bass Inc., Publishers, 350 Sansome Street, San Francisco, California 94104-1342.

SUBSCRIPTIONS for 1994 cost $49.00 for individuals and $72.00 for institutions, agencies, and libraries.

THE MATERIAL in this publication is based on work sponsored wholly or in part by the Office of Educational Research and Improvement, U.S. Department of Education, under contract number RI-93-00-2003. Its contents do not necessarily reflect the views of the Department, or any other agency of the U.S. Government.

EDITORIAL CORRESPONDENCE should be sent to the Editor-in-Chief, Arthur M. Cohen, at the ERIC Clearinghouse for Community Colleges, University of California, 3051 Moore Hall, 405 Hilgard Avenue, Los Angeles, California 90024-1521.

Cover photograph © Rene Sheret, After Image, Los Angeles, California, 1990.

103504

Contents

EDITOR'S NOTES

The economic and educational futures of our nation are growing more and more intertwined. American businesses are facing vast technological and demographic changes while they try to compete in the global marketplace. They have urgent needs for training to remain competitive.

At the same time, colleges are beginning to develop the mechanisms to respond to this urgent training need. They are customizing education and delivering it by contract to local businesses, industries, and government. This customized contract education is often referred to as customized training. At no other time in its history, except during the establishment of the county agent system in the late 1880s, has higher education in general, and community colleges in particular, made such a concerted effort to accommodate business and industry so directly by bringing customized education to the doorsteps of their offices and factories.

Grubb and Stern (1989) found the amount of ferment in this area astounding, indicating both the importance of this subject and the level of creativity that educators and employers are bringing to the effort. The recent national study of customized training by the League for Innovation in the Community College (Doucette, 1993) found that 73.2 percent of the respondents (763 of the 1,042 two-year colleges responding) had programs in place designed to deliver work force training for employees of business, industry, labor, and government. This finding confirmed the emergence of community colleges as important players in the training and retraining of America's work force. Not only are these colleges well positioned geographically to respond to local business, but the development and flexibility of their customized training units promise a timely and appropriate response.

The response to external signals from business is causing internal reflection on and expansion of the community colleges' mission. They are expanding their notion of their markets to include learners who are fully employed in the workplace. Historically, colleges were structured to deliver education to yet-to-be-employed learners—-the future work force. Today, demands from outside the higher education community are causing colleges to expand the continuum of learners to include the fully employed learner in the workplace. Most colleges are not training faculty to teach all along this continuum of learners. Instead, they view fully employed learners as different from "traditional" students and have set up nontraditional programs and systems to deliver customized training. These initiatives are relatively new. According to the League for Innovation in the Community College survey (Doucette, 1993), the majority have come into being within the last five years.

Because programs are still new, there is not yet an abundance of literature about accepted practices that can help administrators and faculty design and deliver customized training. And because the training is customized, future standard practices may be few and far between. What does exist is often anecdotal information (Palmer, 1990).

This volume represents a collection of information and research gathered from some of the foremost leaders and practitioners in the field. It addresses the practical considerations, programs, and strategies that come into play when colleges engage in customized contract training for fully employed learners. The first four chapters deal with managing the enterprise and the structure and systems that expedite that process. The next five chapters provide discussions and examples of exemplary practices and future suggestions for customized contract training. The final chapter lists resources on customized contract training. It is hoped the reader will glean ideas for application as well as policy making in customized training.

Teaching the fully employed learner in the workplace requires considerations that are both similar to and different from those pertinent to teaching the yet-to-be-employed, or traditional, student. In Chapter One, I explore the differences. The adjustments that faculty must make when delivering customized contract training to fully employed learners in the workplace are also addressed. Several examples of faculty development activities that focus on this subject are covered. In Chapter Two, James Jacobs and Debra Bragg share their insights about the conceptual framework and elements that are important when evaluating the outcomes of customized training. In Chapter Three, Nancy Kothenbeutel and Conrad Dejardin address the impact of customized training on the colleges' internal operations, training, and perceptions. Often, customized training is at the cutting edge of education and technology. However, in some institutions, these units are left on the edge and not fully integrated into the mainstream. The authors address this issue. In order for the practitioners to remain at a state-of-the-art level, they need to develop evaluation and training systems. Keeping track of the business side of customized contract training is critical. The management of the information collected and manipulated in customized contract training is addressed in Chapter Four by Maureen H. Ramer and Mike Snowden. They make many practical suggestions for setting up an effective management information system.

The next five chapters address specific strategies and programs. In Chapter Five, Julie Bender and Larry D. Carter explain the collaborative efforts required of businesses. They cite several examples across the country, including the briefing center of the Aurora Economic Development Council located at their local community college. Chapter Six is devoted to the subject of work force literacy and the new directions in which it is going. Bob Cumming explains environmental literacy and assessment. In Chapter Seven, Jack N. Wismer chronicles exemplary training for trade programs across the country that has been developed to help local business as well as traditional students become better prepared for international trade. In Chapter Eight, Jacques

Bernier, Nancy Jackson, and David Moore address the techniques used to conduct a work force environmental assessment. Individual and group interviews, climate surveys, advisory teams, and commitments by management are some of the key elements utilized in the process. Chapter Nine addresses the frontiers of the future. Cary A. Israel takes us on a visionary journey, to where, he believes, customized training should be going in the future. We examine consortia and research roles, learn about intergenerational service programs, and embark on a training path of modernization and virtual reality.

Finally, in Chapter Ten, David Deckelbaum provides an annotated bibliography of ERIC documents on customized contract training. These sources cover a variety of topics, including the planning, promotion, management, and evaluation of programs as well as the building of partnerships between colleges and their communities.

As the education and economic futures of this nation become more intertwined, the need for customized training continues to grow. Examples of the extent and diversity of that customization are now being chronicled (for example, Kantor, 1991). Community colleges that adapt to these needs will be well positioned to provide this training. The American Society of Training and Development reported a decade ago that 90 percent of the nation's companies did their own in-house training. Its 1991 survey showed that 50 percent of all training of existing employees is now provided by external contractors (Doucette, 1993). This is an opportunity for community colleges.

In the process of anticipating and adapting to the expanding work force training needs, community colleges will have to expand their missions to include the fully employed learner in the workplace as a key market segment. This process will require not only a shift in thinking beyond the traditional student but also risk and experimentation. Customized training units can experiment by being incubators for innovation and catalysts for change for both the businesses and the higher education institutions they serve. It is my hope that this volume provides readers and practioners with practical suggestions and insights about how to manage the enterprise and carry out customized training in an exemplary fashion.

Sherrie L. Kantor
Editor

References

Doucette, D. *Community College Workforce Training Programs for Employees of Business, Industry, Labor, and Government: A Status Report.* Laguna Hills, Calif.: League for Innovation in the Community College, 1993. 43 pp. (ED 356 815)

Grubb, W. N., and Stern, D. *Separating the Wheat from the Chaff: The Role of Vocational Education in Economic Development.* Berkeley: National Center for Research in Vocational Education, University of California, Berkeley, 1989. 61 pp. (ED 312 466)

Kantor, S. L. *Direct Services to Businesses Delivered by Colorado Community Colleges.* Denver: Colorado Community College and Occupational Education System, 1991. 43 pp. (ED 343 633)

Palmer, J. "How Do Community Colleges Serve Business and Industry? A Review of Issues Discussed in the Literature." Paper prepared for the American Association of Community and Junior Colleges and the National Alliance of Business, George Mason University, 1990. 62 pp. (ED 319 443)

SHERRIE L. KANTOR *is dean of corporate and continuing education at Central Piedmont Community College, Charlotte, North Carolina. She is former dean of continuing education and community services at Community College of Aurora, Aurora, Colorado.*

*Teaching the fully employed learner in the workplace requires
training and instructional strategies that are different from those
for teaching the yet-to-be-employed learner on the traditional
college campus.*

Training for Customized Training: Learning to Teach the Fully Employed Learner in the Workplace

Sherrie L. Kantor

The boundaries are beginning to blur between the college's more traditional mission of educating learners who are yet to be employed and its expanding mission of educating fully employed learners in the workplace. Enlightened colleges have begun to see the instructional role as a continuum with traditional students on one end and business clients who contract for the training of their employees on the other end. Teaching across the continuum requires training and, at the same time, presents educators with a wonderful opportunity to address a wider variety of subjects, settings, and audiences. Teaching in work settings with fully employed learners not only can update faculty and help keep them exposed to state-of-the-art information and technology but also can serve as an important link to potential jobs for the more traditional or yet-to-be-employed learner.

There are a growing number of faculty development programs that address the skills needed for teaching at one end of the continuum, the traditional yet-to-be-employed learner. However, recent national and state studies (Kantor, 1991) have revealed little to no literature that addresses training for the skills needed to teach the learners on the other end of the continuum—those in business and industry.

Furthermore, the survey of the League for Innovation in the Community College (Doucette, 1993) indicated that one of the biggest obstacles to delivering customized contract training for fully employed learners was the lack of experienced trainers. The survey revealed that the majority of training provided used traditional methods such as lecture and discussion rather than the emerging instructional technologies. The most common staffing pattern was to hire trainers on a contract basis. While there are financial advantages to this pattern, there are also disadvantages to the college. It deprives the college of state-of-the-art information and leaves this important initiative at the periphery of the institution. Participation in contract training by more permanent instructors integrates it into the mainstream where it can be a catalyst in influencing curriculum.

Internships and Hiring Practices Help Expand Faculty Teaching Horizons to Include Customized Training

To increase participation in contract training by full-time faculty it is necessary to reexamine the institution's staffing patterns and remuneration systems as well as its training and incentive systems. For example, Red Rocks Community College in Golden, Colorado, has experimented with faculty internships in the customized training department. The vice president of instruction and the customized training director have worked to make this option available to full-time faculty, and they have done it within the existing structure.

At Central Piedmont Community College in North Carolina, reassignment of "regular" faculty to customized training has begun. For example, they assigned a regular business faculty member to corporate and continuing education for one quarter. The main task was to refine and redevelop the process of assessment and evaluation of business. The development of such tools strengthened customized training as well as the regular business curriculum. The college is developing a full-time customized faculty core with the expertise to complement their client companies' needs and to coordinate the numerous part-time faculty and consultants who participate in the training.

The Community College of Aurora, in Aurora, Colorado, hires full-time customized trainers and managers who have the credentials to teach in both industry and the traditional classroom. While the majority of work is done in industry, these faculty also teach one course each on the traditional end of the continuum. These training managers with faculty contracts are prototypes of future faculty who, with training and institutional support, will be able to teach all along the continuum. This versatility is critical in gaining institutional acceptance of the expanded mission.

Obtaining Training in Customized Training: A Workshop in Partnership with Faculty Development

Partnering with faculty development professionals offers another method for providing training to interested faculty. Customized trainers at six Colorado community colleges organized a training session on customized training for an international faculty development conference in Vail, Colorado, in July 1993. Participants were full-time faculty and faculty development specialists from colleges within and outside the United States. This conference sparked the interest and desire of faculty and faculty development professionals to examine how they could learn to teach along a much broader continuum.

The workshop examined the similarities and differences in teaching the yet-to-be-employed and the fully employed learner. Participants then moved on to implications and strategies that faculty who wish to teach in industry must consider. An active learning simulation exercise was used. The faculty were asked to play the role of a customized trainer interviewing a company representative who is considering the purchase of customized training from the college. The following are highlights of questions considered and implications discovered in relation to the task of teaching fully employed learners.

Student Considerations. The motivation of fully employed learners is an aspect that must be addressed before implementation of training begins. The learners may have chosen to attend the class or they may have been told they must attend by their employer. It is highly recommended that the college establish a training council of representatives from across the company before assessment and training begins. When management lets the college establish a cross-functional team of advisers in setting up the class, there is more of a "buy in" by all parties and it is less likely that the students will feel they "have" to be there.

Fully employed learners often know one another well and this can affect the dynamics of the class. Instructors need to acknowledge and plan activities that consider this familiarity, such as rotating seating and small group assignments frequently. In addition, encouragement of oral or written communication with the instructor on an individual basis should be strongly encouraged. If animosities or rivalries exist among co-workers, written messages give the student a chance to have a more private and authentic dialogue. The instructor must use these strategies and others to establish trust and open communication.

Client Considerations. Another difference in teaching this population is the presence of two clients: the employees as a collective and the employer. Again, the company training council can go a long way in establishing training on which all agree as well as procedures to be used in the delivery of training. For example, it should be made clear that privacy act laws prevent the instructor from posting grades or giving scores to anyone other than the student, so the employer cannot have such information without student permission. Complaints about the class by students must be directed toward the instructor and not the employer. If a complaint cannot be resolved, the training council, which contains a college representative, should be notified. The college needs to be part of the loop when any problems are detected. College representatives should also be notified if instructors have complaints. It needs to be very clear to instructors that the company is a client of the college and not of an individual instructor. With good training and customized state-of-the-art subject matter, the instructor should be aware of the dual audience and able to satisfy both employees and employers.

Subject Matter Considerations. The subject matter in customized training, by its very nature, is based on what the audience "needs to know." This point is important. All effort should be made to design instruction to coincide with a formal or informal assessment of the work force and the workplace. This customization often includes examples and case studies or demonstrations from the workplace. Relevance is key. Application of theory is key. And adaptation to the industry is key.

The outcomes must be measurable and what those outcomes entail should be agreed on at the inception of the program. In addition, upper management and college personnel should agree on and commit to the expected outcomes.

The material must be customized to maximize the effectiveness of the training and its relevance to the company that is purchasing the training. This customization requires careful estimation of the cost of the instructional design or *choreography*, a term coined by Israel (this volume). Such preparation must be built into the price of the contract.

In addition, the instruction and delivery should be adapted to the learning styles of the individual and the company culture. Again, the use of the training council along with learning style assessments will help reveal this information.

Time and Place Considerations. The delivery of instruction must also adapt to the work force schedule. This means that instructors must be willing to deliver training at odd times to accommodate shifts and company priorities. The college's project manager must also be willing to drop in at these odd times to support the efforts. This support is critical. All too often college administrators whose colleges work around the clock do not accommodate their own schedules to acknowledge and support those who work other than the hours of nine to five. Their presence at a five o'clock in the morning shift speaks volumes to company officials and employees as well as to the faculty.

Company schedules may require material to be concentrated, compressed, videotaped, individualized, and delivered in a manner other than that of a ten- or fifteen-week model. A variety of instructional modes may be employed, such as day-long workshops, fiber optic networks, virtual reality simulations, one-to-one consultations, or interactive television. This approach requires faculty who are trained or are willing to be trained to deliver education using these technologies.

Sometimes, development and delivery require a rapid response. Instructors will need to be flexible, knowledgeable, and capable of designing courses in a short period of time. They may be asked to participate in preemployment training where the college conducts screening for start-up or existing training like that done at Pueblo Community College (Zeiss, 1989). Administrators must be willing to cut red tape so that they can proceed without bureaucratic bog-downs. Policies and systems may have to be reevaluated and changed so that they are relevant, expedient, and timely and still accomplish academic integrity. Anthony Zeiss, president of Central Piedmont Community College, advises, "If the system gets in the way, change the system!" (personal communication, August 31, 1993).

Instructional resources must be readily available to accommodate customization in a relatively short period of time. This may require assigning a substitute to allow the classroom teacher with the expertise the time to research and design a class. The payback can be great for both traditional and nontraditional classrooms. Resources must also be available to purchase state-of-the-art materials to deliver just-in-time customized education. Again, the payoff works to the advantage of education and business.

Because 50 percent of most customized training is conducted on site (Doucette, 1993), modifications to the setting may be needed. The training may require ingenuity and flexibility from the instructor. Makeshift flip charts may be needed. A conference room or shop floor may become a classroom, or a seldom-used warehouse corner may suffice for a much needed demonstration. While flexibility is important, balance is also required. The instructor must balance the quality of instruction with the accommodation. If there is too much visual obstruction or the noise level is too high, the instructor will need to inform officials and explain how the site too greatly compromises the experience. The same is true of time. Asking students to learn too much too fast, to sit too long, or to forego assessment can jeopardize effectiveness. The instructor and college need to be forthright about their desire to deliver a quality product that will result in the desired, successful outcome for the company.

Company space offers opportunities as well. It exposes faculty to state-of-the-art technology and information not always available in such an applied way. It contributes to faculty and student transfer of theory to practice. This relevance and application should be built into the instructional design.

Other Training Possibilities and Suggestions

Shadowing of customized trainers by full-time faculty and mentoring by customized trainers are two more ways to increase full-time faculty's awareness of and exposure to this work. The shadowing and mentoring should go both ways. Customized trainers could shadow full-time faculty as well.

Team teaching is another strategy that could be tried. For example, the combination of a full-time faculty member in communications with a customized trainer doing a team exercise for a business would offer both insights.

Partnerships with individuals responsible for faculty development programs can be of great assistance. The approval and buy-in by this group can be extremely valuable. This strategy ensures that faculty can be trained to teach all along the instructional continuum in a systematic fashion.

Similarities with On-Campus Instruction

All of the training characteristics and suggestions mentioned above distinguish customized training from more traditional settings, situations, and delivery styles. While these differences, and strategies for accommodating them, have been addressed, what have not been addressed are the similarities between customized training of fully employed learners and teaching of yet-to-be-employed learners. There are far more similarities than differences. Students in both kinds of settings are, after all, learners, and learning theories that maximize adult learning experiences apply to all of these students. The principles for designing instruction apply to both kinds of settings. In all situations, spatial considerations are part of the planning. The handling of interaction with and inquiry by students inside and outside of the classroom still, of course, occurs for both, as does the rewarding experience of watching students master something new. Faculty need not be intimidated by the differences. With training, whether through mentoring, interning, or a more formal workshop, interested instructors can join in this exciting work. Careful attention to the considerations, implications, and strategies can help ease the transition into customized training experiences. If policies encourage it, administrators create structures that allow it, and training systems develop to facilitate it, more faculty will be able to broaden the continuum along which they teach.

Conclusion

As the mission of community colleges expands to educate learners all along the continuum, including those who are fully employed, the colleges will need to prepare their work force to accommodate that mission. The extent to which a higher education institution engages in training its work force to work in customized training and to expand faculty ability to teach all along a continuum will depend on the institution's commitment to work force training. From commitment will come the resources, creativity, and motivation needed to train the work force within as well as outside the college. This commitment is critical to carrying out the expanded mission of economic development. Clearly, the training will have to be customized to accommodate each college; it is hoped that this chapter provides insights about the need for this training and strategies that might be considered by those who attempt to pursue it.

References

Doucette, D. *Community College Workforce Training Programs for Employees of Business, Industry, Labor, and Government: A Status Report.* Laguna Hills, Calif.: League for Innovation in the Community College, 1993. 43 pp. (ED 356 815)

Kantor, S. L. *Direct Services to Businesses Delivered by Colorado Community Colleges.* Denver: Colorado Community College and Occupational Education System, 1991. 43 pp. (ED 343 633)

Zeiss, A. *Economic Development: A Viewpoint from Business.* Washington, D.C.: National Center for Higher Education, American Association of Community and Junior Colleges, 1989.

SHERRIE L. KANTOR is dean of corporate and continuing education at Central Piedmont Community College, Charlotte, North Carolina. She is former dean of continuing education and community services at Community College of Aurora, Aurora, Colorado.

The conceptual framework described here provides a schema to categorize variables and elements to conduct systematic program evaluation and maintain records that demonstrate the accountability of the two-year postsecondary institution's customized training programs.

The Evaluation of Customized Training

James Jacobs, Debra Bragg

The purpose of this chapter is to present a new conceptual model for evaluation of customized training. By now, most community colleges are performing some type of customized training activity. Yet, for all of this activity, the attempts to evaluate, as opposed to describe, the area of customized activity are still not well developed. It is critical that institutions involved in customized training develop tools for assessing how this activity contributes to their overall missions.

Overview of the Framework

The conceptual framework was developed to describe the key components of customized training. The framework provides a schema for categorizing sets of variables and elements that can be used to (1) conduct systematic program evaluation of customized training, with the goals of improving programs and assessing impact, and (2) develop and maintain records that demonstrate the accountability of the two-year postsecondary institution's customized training programs.

The conceptual framework contains sets of variables associated with context, process, and outcomes. The level and scope of detail of information needed to collect data for each set of variables depend on the nature of the customized training program and the purpose of that evaluation. The sets of variables are broken down into illustrative elements to help provide a comprehensive description of information that can be collected to describe the nature, extent, and impact of customized training. Figure 2.1 provides an overview of the major categories of variables designated as context, process, and outcomes in the conceptual framework.

NEW DIRECTIONS FOR COMMUNITY COLLEGES, no. 85, Spring 1994   © Jossey-Bass Publishers

Figure 2.1. Conceptual Framework for Evaluating Customized Training

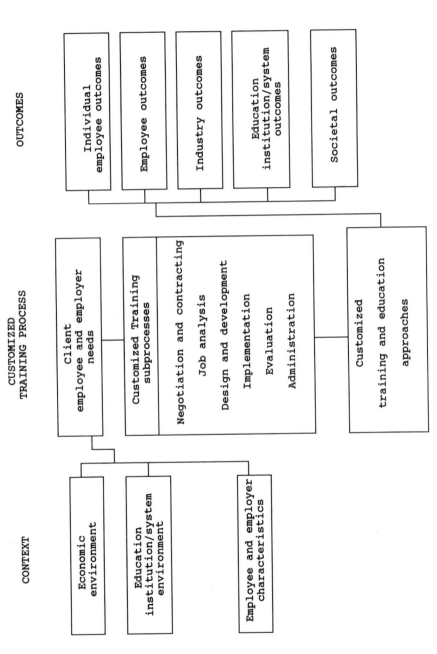

Context for Customized Training

Context reflects the characteristics of states, communities, institutions, and clients that influence the way in which customized training processes are carried out (see Table 2.1). Further, the sets of variables associated with context help describe the environment for customized training as well as give perspective to understanding the outcomes that accrue to individuals, firms and agencies, and clients; to two-year postsecondary institutions as service providers; and to society as a whole as a result of customized training. This part of the conceptual framework helps us to understand the array of characteristics within the environment of and the context for customized training.

The context for customized training is viewed as composed of three categories of variables: economic environment, educational institutions and systems, and employee and employer characteristics. Each of these sets of contextual variables consists of elements that describe the environment in which customized training is conducted.

Economic Environment. Economic environment is the first set of contextual variables. Economic environment identifies the past, current, and projected future conditions of the international, national, state, and local economies. This set of variables provides a description of the economic setting in which customized training is conducted. The conceptual framework proposes that four sets of illustrative elements related to economic environment be evaluated. The first set consists of indicators of international, national, state, and local economic conditions, such as international, national, state and local unemployment rates; trends in gross national product; local business volume; and national, state, and local average income levels.

Table 2.1. Contextual Variables for Evaluation of Customized Training

Contextual Variables	Illustrative Elements
Economic environment	Indicators of international, national, state, and local economic conditions
	Government economic development policies and programs
	State characteristics
	Community characteristics
Educational institutions and systems	Education system policies, programs, and practices
	Two-year institutional policies, programs, and practices
	Customized training unit administrative organizational structure, policies, programs, and practices
Employee and employer characteristics	Characteristics of organizational (employer) clients
	Characteristics of individual (employee) clients
	Relationships between two-year institutions and clients

Government policies and programs in the area of economic development are the second set of elements related to the economic environment. This category of elements provides information about the specific federal, state, and local policies and programs employed to stimulate the economy. Job training programs funded at the federal or state level, such as the Job Training Partnership Act or its state-level equivalents, are examples of programs designed to stimulate economic development through improvements in work force competence. When collecting information regarding government economic development policies and programs, it is important to identify the purpose and scope of each of the various strategies used. It is also critical to determine in what ways the strategies may be competing or conflicting, thereby impeding opportunities for economic development. For example, a strategy to attract new business for an area may conflict with the policies to retain present firms.

The third and fourth sets of elements identified in association with the economic environment are characteristics of the state and local community. Similar information needs to be collected in relationship to these two entities. This information includes the demographic characteristics of the populations, types of dominant businesses and industries, labor supply, and work force skill levels. It is important to examine trends in these data to determine how the economic environment of specific states and communities has changed over previous years and is likely to change in the future.

Educational Institutions and Systems. The second set of variables identified as part of the context for customized training is the area of educational institutions and systems. This set of variables describes the past, current, and future state of educational systems and the characteristics of two-year postsecondary institutions and customized training units within them. This category of variables examines the scope and purpose of the various educational institutions and systems in relationship to economic development and customized training.

The first set of illustrative elements identified as part of educational institutions and systems is described as the policies, programs, and practices of educational systems. The category of educational systems refers to the federal-, state-, and local-level systems of public or private educational organizations at the secondary and postsecondary levels. Examples of the information that needs to be analyzed in the area of educational systems and economic development include the missions, philosophical perspectives, historical involvement, administrative structures, leadership commitment, and span of control of the educational systems in relationship to economic development and, more specifically, customized training. It is useful to examine the ways in which the missions and goals of educational systems conflict or compete in meeting economic development goals.

The second set of elements associated with educational institutions and systems is characteristics of the two-year postsecondary educational institutions' policies, programs, and practices. Examples of information that needs to be collected about two-year postsecondary institutions are the level of leadership commitment to customized training within the institution; the nature of decision-making processes concerning customized training (for example, centralized, decentralized, or integrated); the level of support for customized training from departments across the college (for example, broad-based or narrow-based support); the nature of mission statements, including focus on economic development; and the level of institutional flexibility enabling customized training programs to be responsive to the needs of external clients.

The third set of elements describes the customized training unit. Examples of information that is needed to help describe context in this area are the administrative and organizational structure of the customized training unit; leadership commitment to meeting economic development objectives; and the responsiveness of the unit's internal policies, practices, and programs in meeting client needs. It is also important to determine a unit's internal organizational structure and processes (for example, design, development, and implementation) in order to understand the ways in which external client needs are identified and addressed.

Employee and Employer Characteristics. The third set of contextual variables concerns information about employees and their employers as external clients of customized training programs. This set of variables constitutes the characteristics of individuals, private sector organizations, public sector agencies, and other types of institutions that receive customized training products and services in exchange for payments to the two-year postsecondary institutions.

The first set of elements associated with employee and employer characteristics is the characteristics of individual clients (that is, employees). This category of illustrative elements provides an overall description of the nature of individual employees who are typically served in customized training programs. Examples of information needed in relation to employees are age, educational level, and occupational level. In addition to this information, it is important to obtain an understanding of the general nature of the job performance deficiencies of employees in order to design a relevant training program.

The second set of illustrative elements related to employee and employer characteristics is the characteristics of organizational clients (that is, employers). This set of elements provides a description of public and private organizations that have historically sought and are currently seeking customized training. Examples of the type of information that would be collected in relationship to this set of elements include the types of businesses, industries, or public agencies; the size of firms or agencies; the types of occupations employed in the work force; the types of technologies utilized; the level of involvement of labor unions; and the general nature of work force skill requirements.

Finally, a third set of illustrative elements is the relationship between two-year postsecondary institutions and external clients. It is important to obtain information about both the historical and the present nature of relationships that exist between institutions and clients in the delivery of any training or education services, especially customized training. Within this set of elements, it is also important to discern the scope and nature of these prior and current partnerships. Examples of the information that is needed include descriptions of partnerships that have occurred, assessments of the quality and effectiveness of previous partnerships, and the level of cooperation and coordination associated with previous and current partnerships. Without doubt, the history of the partnerships affects current and future customized training programs.

Customized Training Process

The customized training process involves the entire scope of administrative and operational subprocesses involved in producing and delivering the various customized training approaches (see Table 2.2). Through the subprocesses (for example, designing, developing, and evaluating), customized training programs evolve. It is necessary to understand these subprocesses to determine their importance in producing customized training programs and to assess the relationship of process to outcomes. The customized training process in its most rudimentary form is composed of three sets of variables that form the components of the customized training process.

Client Needs Assessment. The first variable identifies client needs as the starting point for the customized training process. Client needs may be identified by the employer or through a formal needs assessment activity. Often, clients do not know the extent and nature of the training needs of their employees and rely heavily on the institutions to identify and design cus-

Table 2.2. Process Variables for Evaluation of Customized Training

Process Variables	Illustrative Elements
Client needs assessment	Needs assessment to identify academic knowledge and skills, technical knowledge and skills, and managerial knowledge and skills
Customized training subprocesses	Negotiation and contracting Job analysis Design and development Implementation Evaluation Administration
Customized training and education approaches	Client-driven custom-designed training courses Modification of training or education courses Alternative delivery of training courses Training courses for special populations

tomized training programs that will enable them to reach desired goals like increased productivity and profits. The intent of identifying client needs is to recognize employee performance deficiencies that require remediation through an education or training program (see Cumming, this volume; Bernier, Jackson, and Moore, this volume, for more on assessment).

Customized Training Subprocesses. The second set of process variables identifies the phases of development of customized training, defined in this conceptual framework as the customized training subprocesses. It is important to obtain an understanding of the way in which these subprocesses are executed to produce particular approaches to customized training. These subprocesses are negotiation and contracting, job analysis, design and development, implementation, evaluation, and administration.

It is important to collect information related to the relevance, efficiency, and cost of execution of the various subprocesses. Through data collection activities, institutions can identify ways in which subprocesses produce customized training programs that result in specific outcomes for individual employees, employers, educational institutions, and society. These data can also help two-year institutions structure internal organizational and administrative processes to facilitate efficient delivery of customized training programs.

Customized Training and Education Approaches. The third set of process variables includes the customized training and education approaches that evolve from the six subprocesses. These approaches are grouped into four categories: client-driven and custom-designed training courses, modification of training or education courses, alternative delivery of training courses, and training courses for special populations. They can be used independently or jointly to describe many activities identified as part of customized training.

When obtaining information about the various customized training and education approaches, it is important to establish a set of criteria that can be used to determine the overall quality of the programs from the perspective of the stakeholders, in this case, the external client, as well as the two-year postsecondary institutions. Criteria that can be used to determine the quality of customized training include originality, appropriateness, job relevance, specificity, comprehensiveness, flexibility, responsiveness, accuracy, timeliness, and cost benefits.

Outcomes of Customized Training

Finally, outcomes are associated with the various target groups for customized training (see Table 2.3). The framework identifies the specific types of outcomes that are likely to occur for individuals, firms and agencies, educational institutions or systems, and society as a consequence of high-quality customized training programs. Gaining a better understanding of the ways in which customized training influences these outcomes is important. The sets of outcomes variables are categorized as follows.

Table 2.3. Outcomes Variables for Evaluation of Customized Training

Outcomes Variables	Illustrative Elements
Individual employee outcomes	Competence development Financial reward Career development or advancement Job satisfaction
Employer outcomes	Productivity and profits Stability Expansion Adaptability Employee morale
Industry outcomes	Spillover benefits among similar firms in productivity and profits, stability, expansion, adaptability, and employee morale
Educational institution or system outcomes	Profit Change in two-year institution programs, policies, and practices Change in relationships between two-year institutions and clients
Societal outcomes	Economic development Quality of life

Individual Employee Outcomes. The first set of outcomes variables is described as individual employee outcomes. These outcomes variables may occur for individual employees as a result of their participation in customized training programs. The first set of illustrative elements within employee outcomes is in the area of competence development, including competencies in academic, technical, and managerial areas. The second set of illustrative elements describes individual employee outcomes in terms of financial reward, including higher wages and better benefits.

The third set of elements relates to employees' opportunities for career development or advancement and alternative or improved employment opportunities as a result of involvement in customized training programs. Finally, the fourth set of elements relates to job satisfaction. Information collected about job satisfaction can provide a means of determining the ways in which customized training influences individual employee satisfaction with a job or overall employment situation. Customized training may also increase the ability of the two-year institution to act as an arm of government to respond to the interests of business and thereby respond to major constituencies in the community. In this way, customized training can become a component in the overall human resources strategy of government.

Employer Outcomes. The second set of outcome variables is associated with the employer. Evaluation information is needed regarding this second category of outcomes variables to obtain an understanding of the benefits that accrue to private firms, public agencies, and other client organizations as a result of customized training programs. The first set of elements relates to the area of enhanced productivity and profits for the organization. It is important to determine the ways in which customized training contributes to productivity and profits, including the ways in which the collective improvement of employee competence and productivity influence production levels, the ways internal training costs are lowered by using two-year institutions to deliver customized training, and the changes in competitive position resulting from customized training programs.

Another important element of employer outcomes is the stability of employer organizations within particular communities, states, or regions of the country. Information about changes in the competence of the work force, turnover rates, or productivity levels related to customized training programs is important. A third element associated with employer outcomes is expansion of business and industry. This element identifies the extent to which economic growth for particular firms or agencies can be related to customized training.

Similarly, the fourth element identifies the area of adaptability, including the ability of a firm or agency to meet the needs of its identified client groups. It is important to determine the extent to which firms and agencies have increased flexibility to deliver different products and services as a result of their employees' participation in customized training. The fifth element associated with employer outcomes is employee morale. This element provides evidence of the collective attitudes of employees toward the employer and the overall work environment. Any changes in employee morale, such as reductions in complaints or adversities, that result from customized training programs are important to identify to better understand employer outcomes.

Industry Outcomes. This third set of outcomes is associated with businesses and industries that are grouped due to their proximity, similarity in purpose, or partnership relationships. Small business supplier relationships that exist with larger industrial firms are an example of the nature of the organizations addressed with this set of outcomes. Generally, the set of elements associated with employer outcomes—productivity and profits, stability, expansion, adaptability, and morale—provide a means of describing the outcomes for groups of business and industrial firms as well.

Educational Institution or System Outcomes. The fourth set of outcomes variables relates to changes in the two-year postsecondary educational institution or system as as result of the involvement in offering customized training to external clients. The first set of elements that describes the educational institutions or systems is associated with profit, specifically, the revenues that institutions receive from subsidized or nonsubsidized programs.

The second set of elements surrounds the area of change in two-year postsecondary educational institutions' or systems' policies, programs, or practices in relationship to their involvement in customized training. Examples of information needed related to this set of elements are changes in staffing, curricula, enrollments, job placement services for graduates, institutional missions, responsiveness to community needs, and relationships to private and public organizations within communities, states, and regions of the country.

A third set of elements associated with educational institution and system outcomes is related to the changes that occur in the relationships between two-year postsecondary institutions and external clients. It is important to determine whether customized training stimulates improvements in the types of partnerships that occur between institutions and clients involved in the programs. Examples of information that could be used to identify positive changes in relationships include evidence of increased enrollment of employees of external client organizations in other, traditional programs offered by two-year institutions; heightened involvement of employees of external client organizations in curriculum development and improvement efforts; priority hiring for graduates of two-year postsecondary programs; increases in internships or apprenticeships for two-year postsecondary students; and increases in equipment donations.

Societal Outcomes. The first set of outcomes variables examines the benefit of customized training to society as a whole. The intent of this set of outcomes is to identify outcomes pertinent to individual citizens, communities, and states. Within the area of societal outcomes, it is important to identify elements of economic conditions of the community and state that may be influenced by the customized training programs provided by two-year institutions. Information collected in relationship to economic condition can be used to describe changes in the local, state, or regional economy that can potentially be attributed to customized training programs. Examples of these elements are property values, community support for education, economic growth, economic stability, employment rates, local business volume, tax rates, average salary levels, percentage of the community living on public assistance, and services provided for specific companies (that is, inducement programs).

Finally, a second set of elements related to societal outcomes describes information related to changes in the quality of life for citizens in a particular community or state where customized training is conducted. Although these elements are difficult to measure, they are important to examine in order to gain an understanding of the impact of customized training on society as a whole. Examples of information that could be collected to assist in describing quality of life are the changes that occur in social climate, political stability, environmental services, government services, law enforcement, infrastructures, school systems, and overall enhancement of the skilled work force in the community.

Conclusion: Toward a National Role for Customized Training

In the original formulation of the above model, there was little role for evaluation of customized training as part of a national program for work force development. However, with the advent of President Clinton's administration, there appears to be a new interest in the federal agenda for community colleges. A document prepared by the transition team for the administration introduced the concept of a national associate's degree. At the National Institute of Standards and Technology, there is increasing recognition of the role of community colleges in the formation of the Manufacturing Extension Program, a federal attempt to modernize small- and medium-size firms. Finally, in the legislation calling for the development of national skill standards, there is language relating to the role of community colleges in the development of these standards (for a discussion of these developments, see Dervarics, 1993).

These activities raise an important new perspective for community college practitioners. Where once success was measured by the work within one industry, or, even more minutely, with one firm, now the measurement must be how well the aggregate training offered through the community colleges serves to maintain and strengthen the base of American industry.

At this time, we have no easy way to perform this type of evaluation. However, a few general points can be made regarding the performance of the community colleges: (1) Successful community colleges will be those that can work together with other work force development institutions to aid their clients. (2) Successful community colleges will be those that can work with other community colleges in offering a system of services to firms. (3) Successful community colleges will be those that recognize that the delivery of classroom training is only one aspect of work force development from a national perspective.

In large part, training must be embedded in the general process of firm modernization. This means that community colleges need to engage in assessment of firms, aid in achieving technical knowledge on process and product, and contribute to many other areas that heretofore have not been part of the activities of these colleges. It also means that some of the skilled training and development is best performed on-site by the workers themselves. The role of the community college will be the hub of the learning process, wherever it occurs.

These are only beginning stages as the federal agenda begins to develop. They assume that customized training will remain a function of the community colleges as part of their self-definition. They also assume that the colleges as a group have a role today in the national agenda. This is not a closed question. Community colleges are products of local conditions, typically run by local boards of trustees who see their communities' needs as paramount. For community colleges to be successful in the national arena, they need to take seriously the national issue of work force development and determine how as a system they can best intervene. Then this activity, emerging out of the work over the past fifteen years, will become the opening for a real national agenda of the community colleges in their evolution as institutions.

Reference

Dervarics, G. "How to Give Students Job Skills." *Technical and Skills Training,* July 1993, pp. 20–23.

JAMES JACOBS is director of policy research at Macomb Community College, Warren, Michigan.

DEBRA BRAGG is assistant professor in the Department of Vocational and Technical Education, College of Education, University of Illinois, Urbana-Champaign.

Although customized training programs are often at the cutting edge of education and technology, customized training units are not always fully integrated into the mainstream of the colleges' internal operations.

Contract Training: Avoiding the Rodney Dangerfield Syndrome by Practicing Good Internal Marketing

Nancy Kothenbeutel, Conrad Dejardin

From our perspectives, Rodney Dangerfield's "I don't get no respect" theme applies to the community services and continuing education function of the community college as much as, from the perspective of others, it applies to the customized training function, or what can be called *contract training* or *economic development*. Furthermore, there are a number of arguments presented in this volume to support our belief that the contract training function belongs in the community services and continuing education unit of the community college. So while this volume is intended to address the contract training function, we address internal relationships from a broader perspective.

The assigned topic of our chapter surprised us. When we sat down to discuss how we would approach the topic, we kept asking each other, Why, after all this time, is the matter of respect for adult and community education still an issue? A comprehensive community college consists of three divisions: community services and continuing education, arts and sciences, and vocational technical education. Either we as professionals believe in the comprehensive community college or we do not. If we do, then we must acknowledge that all divisions of the community college have value. If we do not, then we should reevaluate our commitment to the philosophy of the community college.

It is our contention that the issue of respect as professionals is a far greater issue internally than externally. Our external customers assume we are professionals. Business and industry are far more concerned about receiving top-quality, easily accessible education and training at a price they can afford than they are about our status within our institutions. Our more traditional students want the same thing. Why then are community services and continuing education administrators more conscious of how they are perceived internally than are other administrators of major divisions within the college?

Ireland, Smydra, and Tucker (1988) cited a 1987 national survey of community services and continuing education administrators and presidents in noting that, "Over the last few years the status of the community services and continuing education function, in terms of prominence and impact, had increased in 69% of the institutions and was maintained in another 21% of the responding colleges" (pp. 2–3). It sometimes seems as though we fail to believe what we are told. Could it be that we are our own worst enemies? Perhaps it is time to ask ourselves, "Is it them, or is it us?"

History and Mission of Community Services and Continuing Education

In "A Policy Statement of the National Council on Community Services and Continuing Education," Ireland, Smydra, and Tucker (1988, pp. 5–6) defined community services and continuing education as follows:

> That community college function that goes beyond traditional transfer, vocational, and general education to effect lifelong learning of the general citizenry. . . . Community services and continuing education has as its major components civic literacy, work force training and retraining, cultural enrichment, and community resource development. All courses, programs, and activities provided to implement the various components have as their objective imparting knowledge, developing skills, or clarifying values. The approach or delivery mode is one that enables the citizenry to access quality programs and needed competencies any time, any place, and in a format that blends education with work and leisure time pursuits throughout life. Implementation is achieved through experimentation and community collaboration in the broadest sense of community, within and outside the institution.

Also in 1988, the Commission on the Future of Community Colleges outlined academic goals for community colleges throughout the nation. One of those goals is that "the community college should make available to adults a rich array of short term and continuing education courses to encourage lifelong learning and help students meet their social, civic, and career obligations" (Commission on the Future of Community Colleges, 1988, p. 15). In addition, the Commission stated that "every community college should work with employers to develop a program of recurrent education to keep the work force up-to-date and well-educated. Such a strategy should become an integral part of any regional economic development program" (p. 23).

The community services and continuing education professional has been involved in training, retraining, and upgrading the work force for many years. The two aforementioned documents helped reinforce the idea that contract training is a legitimate community college function. They gave new credence to the activity of contracting with a particular industry to provide training to meet specific company goals and objectives, as opposed to more general learning for the "public good." This legitimacy was further reinforced by Maiuri (1993, p. 7): "A well educated and trained workforce can assist a community in its ability to attract new business and, more important, can assist in the retention and expansion of existing business and industry." That many states have enacted legislation to support economic development through job training has supported increased activity in the area of contract training through the community college.

Provision of contract training is not enough. The services must be effective. The Iowa Department of Education (1991) studied the impact of customized training within the state of Iowa and found that the businesses and industries that utilized contract training services provided through the community colleges were overwhelmingly pleased with the quality of these services. That same study concluded, "The continuing education programs offered through Iowa's community colleges have had a significant impact on economic development strategies and the overall quality of life currently enjoyed by Iowa citizens" (p. 8).

Contract Training and Organizational Structure

As professionals in the field, our place in the organizational hierarchy impacts both our perceptions of ourselves and the perceptions of our colleagues about us. No other division within the community college system has had such an impact, either for better or worse, on the image of the college within the community. Business and industry, both large and small, spend thousands of dollars on upgrading the skills of their work forces. They expect, and deserve, to receive the highest quality education for the dollars they spend. A positive relationship with the businesses and industries who spend their training dollars with the community college can pay rich dividends. It can enhance the perception of the college in general and perhaps even generate credit enrollments. A negative relationship can be difficult, if not impossible, to overcome.

A 1993 study conducted by the League for Innovation in the Community College identified obstacles faced by those responsible for contract training within the community college system (Doucette, 1993). Lack of financial support was the most commonly cited major obstacle in providing work force training. Another obstacle, identified as minor, was the lack of recognition and support internally, particularly from the faculty. It is our contention that these obstacles can be overcome by offering contract training services through an existing division within the college. By offering this training through an existing division, the function is enhanced by the fact that there is an organizational structure in place to provide adequate support, both human and fiscal.

In addition, by placing the contract training function within an existing unit, the rest of the institution is better able to understand how this training function is organized, funded, implemented, and evaluated. A lack of understanding in this area may lead others within the institution to question the quality of the contract training. It may also lead to the perception that contract training diverts scarce resources from the rest of the institution. This perception can prove disastrous to internal marketing efforts.

A separate unit, even if it reports directly to the chief executive officer (CEO), may lack both financial as well as faculty support. It may also lack the support of other administrators within the institution. Finally, the positioning of contract training services as part of an existing unit's operation lessens the impact of the possibly tenuous nature of that particular type of programming effort. For example, the management-by-objectives movement was very strong a number of years ago, yet it is not at all in vogue today. The same concept may apply to the current quality movement and the terminology that applies to it. No one would question the quality movement, the need for quality in business and industry (or education for that matter). However, some of that terminology may exist for a period of time and then fade away in favor of some more popular concept, terminology, or movement. Contract training should be positioned in such a way that it becomes an integral and ongoing part of the services offered by the community college and thus less subject to the ebb and flow of social fads.

The community services and continuing education program, the arts and sciences program, and the vocational technical program that make up the primary divisions of the community college system provide stability for the contract training function. It behooves us to attach to those existing units new educational programs that result from our efforts to respond to community needs. It is clear that contract training services for business and industry should be attached to the existing unit that has the most experience in working directly with business and industry, and that is most flexible in its ability to respond. That unit is the community services and continuing education unit. Most community colleges appear to recognize that fact. The aforementioned study by the League for Innovation in the Community College found that over 90 percent (Doucette, 1993, p. iv) of the customized training programs operating in the community colleges surveyed were administered by the dean or director of community services and continuing education.

At Eastern Iowa Community College District, contract training began in earnest in 1985. The responsibility for this training was assumed by those individuals within the community services and continuing education division who, prior to that time, had been responsible for noncredit offerings to the general public in the areas of business, trade and industry, and management. The Business and Industry Center was established as a separate department within the community services and continuing education division. This division reports to an executive director, who reports to the CEO.

At Eastern Iowa Community College District, contract training is expected to be financially self-sufficient, which is defined as the capability of covering all the direct costs of instructors and materials as well as the indirect costs of professional staff who coordinate and implement the program, support staff, office supplies, and marketing. This self-sufficiency is achieved through fees for service. Any dollars generated in excess of these base expenses are returned to the general fund for use by the institution as a whole.

Contract training at Eastern Iowa Community College District is evaluated in a number of ways. Every student has the opportunity to evaluate both course content and the instructors at the conclusion of any program of study. The results of these evaluations are taken very seriously by program coordinators and influence the content of future courses as well as instructor selection. In addition, program coordinators work closely with the contracting industry in curriculum development to ensure that there is mutual agreement between Eastern Iowa Community College District and the industry on course goals and objectives. Contact is maintained with the contracting industry throughout the training program. Eastern Iowa Community College District contract training staff want to know whether or not behavioral changes are observed on the job. In other words, are program participants using what they learned? Follow-up is done on an informal basis after the training concludes to gauge the lasting effects of the training.

Finally, at Eastern Iowa Community College District, close attention is paid to repeat business. Customers who feel positive about the services they received come back.

Another example of how a training program for business and industry can develop through the community services and continuing education unit of the community college occurred at Iowa Valley Community College District. When a major manufacturing company announced its intention to consolidate two of its plants either in Marshalltown, Iowa, site of its Plant A, or another city in another midwestern state where it operated Plant B, or possibly in a different location altogether, the mayor of Marshalltown created a task force to work on devising ways to encourage the company to select Marshalltown as the site. The selection would mean the addition of five hundred to six hundred jobs to the Marshalltown work force, and certainly a major boost to the economy of this central Iowa community of twenty-five thousand.

The mayor asked the community college vice president for community services and continuing education to serve on this task force, knowing that the new workers would require extensive training, and knowing that any company making a decision on relocation would certainly review the quality of education at that new location. The community services and continuing education record of community involvement demonstrated responsiveness and experience in providing education and training programs for business and industry, and the well-being of the community in general was certainly a factor in this appointment.

Fifteen to twenty community leaders worked cooperatively to develop an economic incentive package that obviously, in the end, helped to persuade the company officials to select Marshalltown as the site for their consolidation. The community college's community services and continuing education part of this package included a $3 million training program funded through the Iowa Industrial New Jobs Training Program.

The vice president of community services and continuing education called on the college's business development center and the associate dean for business assistance services to develop the actual training program. Working with the manufacturing company's CEO and human resources director, a complete training program was developed, which will be conducted over a three-year period. Approximately one-half of the project will include on-the-job training, and the other half will be what is referred to as *hard training* (in the classroom or laboratory, at the college, or on-site). Individual training plans will be developed for each new employee. The college will add the position of coordinator-instructor to work specifically on this project, and this individual will work with the company's human resources and training director to help bring the resources of the college to bear on fulfilling the company's training needs and thus enhance the training program over the duration of the Industrial New Jobs Training Program and beyond.

Clearly, this training project should give the company an edge among its competitors. Quality and productivity will be enhanced. The company's opportunity for success is significantly enhanced. The community college is fulfilling its role of being close to the community, of providing quality education and training, and of doing all of this in partnership with the company and the community.

Interest of the CEO

The importance of the community services and continuing education division and the visibility of the contract training function are sufficient to warrant having the division head report directly to the CEO of the institution. This sends a message to the rest of the institution that the division is a significant part of the community college.

Internal Marketing

Community services and continuing education professionals want good internal relationships. But these relationships should not be a primary goal. The overriding goal should be to provide quality educational experiences at affordable prices. That is valuable to the customer and valuable to the institution.

Contract training has internal customers and external customers. The external customers are the industries served and the internal customers are the other divisions in the colleges that provide services to us, and vice versa. Internal customers should maintain an awareness of one another's needs and try to meet those needs in a professional way.

It is important for the community services and continuing education administrator of contract training to market the programs internally to the extent that all employees of the community college perceive them as a necessary service that is provided in a quality manner. One cannot expect people from outside the community college to see those programs as quality if they are not so perceived internally.

Contract training is a unique function within the institution, and, as such, communication is more important in this area than in the more traditional divisions of the college. The CEO and others within the institution are often very active in the community. It is essential to inform the other division heads and the CEO about the training projects under way in the division. This practice prevents them from being caught off-guard and embarrassed. No one likes to meet someone from industry only to have them discuss a training program that the college employee knows nothing about.

It is also important to take advantage of opportunities to link contract training activities with the rest of the institution. This means going beyond service on committees and willingness to help other divisions with staffing and so on. Community services and continuing education administrators must be ready to allow contract training to be used as a means of revitalizing the credit faculty by utilizing them as instructors where appropriate. Department chairs should be invited into the contract training classes to present information about other opportunities available through the community college.

If our colleagues are to value and appreciate community services and continuing education and the contract training function, they must be told not only what we do but why it is done. To say it is a part of the mission is not enough, particularly in a time of scarce resources. The administrator must take the time to explain how contract training fits with the more traditional aspects of the college, that is, the vocational technical programs and the arts and sciences programs. The education and training options, including contract training, available through the community services and continuing education division allow adults to find employment, seek better jobs, or maintain their current jobs. Faculty must understand that training, retraining, and upgrading of worker skills through technical training, development of basic skills, and development of critical thinking and problem-solving skills increase worker productivity, improve the quality of life within the community, and build a better economic base for the community.

If the training provided helps business and industry compete more successfully in a global economy, then this part of the community college mission has been fulfilled. In working directly with business and industry, or other types of service agencies, the community services and continuing education division maintains close contact with the external community. Significant and effective linkages of local community entities (businesses, industries, local educational agencies, and so on) are developed in an effort to expand the division's programming base. This expansion is valuable for both the community and the college. The businesses and industries have better-trained workers who are more productive, which improves profitability and stabilizes the economic base of the local community. At the same time, the community college increases its awareness of new industrial procedures and practices. When this information is communicated to the rest of the college, program development efforts can be enhanced, instructors can more easily maintain an awareness of current practices in their fields, and, finally, ideas can be tested prior to their introduction into the credit curriculum. The planning process for the college as a whole is also facilitated.

Internal marketing of customized training programs is not a great deal different from the marketing of any other aspect of the education enterprise. From a broad standpoint, the community college would be most effective if all employees were kept informed, to the greatest extent possible, about all of the activities of the college. This is particularly true for the successful activities on which people can build pride by recognizing both the importance of the activities and their part in them. People need to have the feeling of ownership. They need to have the feeling of belonging. They need to understand the ins and outs of the decision-making process, and they need to have a role in making those decisions.

The need for internal marketing of the customized training program should not be overemphasized at the expense of other programs. However, community services and continuing education professionals are invariably guilty of focusing so intensely on getting a job done that they forget to tell colleagues about it. Community services and continuing education professionals need to ensure that people understand that work done in industry and the relationships that are built have a positive impact on the college as a whole. A community college graduate applying to an industry for a position is more likely to be received in a positive manner if the industry has had positive experiences with the contract training unit of the college. The converse of this situation could also happen, and that must be recognized as well.

Community services and continuing education administrators need to be persistent in their efforts to inform others within the institution of the activities, successes, and extent of involvement with business and industry in contract training. There are times when it appears that this information is not getting across. People are in their own worlds and have their own areas of responsibility. It is the responsibility of the community services and continuing education administrators to encourage others to think outside of their own boundaries and to consider the broadest range of services of the community college. To achieve this goal, these administrators must persist in their efforts and take every opportunity to talk with faculty or other units of the institution. The same holds true for the president and the dean of instruction or vice president of instruction, who need to accept their responsibilities and engage in this internal marketing effort as well. The communication process may change depending on the internal customer. For example, community services and continuing education administrators can provide lists of those businesses and industries that have developed contract training relationships with the college to college-internal customers, such as the head of the foundation or the head of alumni, before these heads proceed with fundraising efforts. A positive, supportive relationship may already have been established with the college through contract training programs, which college fundraisers can exploit.

Faculty members need to understand that the relationship with industry is more than twice-a-year advisory committee meetings. Rather, the relationship entails ongoing daily contact and in-depth analysis of the processes that are used in the industrial environment. Through sharing with faculty, programs can be updated to maintain currency.

An aspect of the community college that we need to continue to exploit is its community-based nature. Many observers have written that the community services and continuing education unit provides that community-based characteristic to the community college. Community services and continuing education professionals need to guard against the elitism that comes from thinking of the college as separate from, or above, the community. That can be done through continuing efforts to make involvement with business and industry a high priority.

This priority is consistent with a report of the National Center on Education and the Economy (1990), which, in its conclusion, expressed concern for the practice of continuing to define educational success as "time in the seat" rather than developing a new system that focuses on the demonstrated achievement of high standards. As the United States struggles to maintain its status as a world leader and enhance its ability to compete with other countries whose educational efforts may be substantially greater than ours, community colleges have an essential role to play through training and retraining programs that serve the work force through business and industry. The concept of lifelong learning must continue to be applied. Adults as well as children are continually in the learning process. We must recognize that not everyone will complete four years of college. People need to be trained for employment, and they will need to continue to be trained and retrained at their places of work if they are to maintain the skills required of today's high-technology businesses and industries.

Conclusion

Does the community services and continuing education administrator market internally in a different way from other college administrators? To some extent, yes, but not too differently. As professionals in a community college environment, we have an obligation to inform our colleagues of what is being done and why. Others should be treated with dignity and respect—just as we want to be treated. If community services and continuing education administrators concentrate on doing their job well, perhaps this issue will cease to be an issue at all.

References

Commission on the Future of Community Colleges. *Building Communities: A Vision for a New Century.* Washington, D.C.: American Association of Community and Junior Colleges, 1988. 58pp. (ED 293 578)

Doucette, D. *Community College Workforce Training Programs for Employees of Business, Industry, Labor, and Government: A Status Report.* Laguna Hills, Calif.: League for Innovation in the Community College, 1993. 43 pp. (ED 356 815)

Iowa Department of Education. *A Study of the Impact of Iowa Community College Continuing Education Programs.* Des Moines: Iowa Department of Education, 1991. 137 pp. (ED 331 560)

Ireland, J., Smydra, M., and Tucker, N. *The Continuing Mission and Future Role of Community Services and Continuing Education in Community, Technical, and Junior Colleges: A Policy Statement of the National Council on Community Services and Continuing Education.* Washington, D.C.: National Council on Community Services and Continuing Education, 1988. 13 pp. (ED 309 816)

Maiuri, G. M. "Economic Development: What Is the Community College's Responsibility? The Role of Contract and Continuing Education." *Community Services Catalyst,* 1993, 23 (1), 7–8.

National Center on Education and the Economy. *America's Choice: High Skills or Low Wages.* Rochester, N.Y.: National Center on Education and the Economy, 1990. 209 pp. (ED 323 297)

NANCY KOTHENBEUTEL is executive director of continuing education and contract training, Eastern Iowa Community College District.

CONRAD DEJARDIN is vice president of continuing education and community services, Iowa Valley Community College District.

An ideal information system for contract education program managers is proposed and a current model is described that enables a program operator to measure the impact of the program, provide summary data, and communicate with other providers.

Using a Management Information System Effectively for Contract Education Programs

Maureen H. Ramer, Mike Snowden

As program managers, are we able to develop an annual business plan as a result of data from the previous year's performance? Are we able to manage the financial aspects of our operation? Are we able to identify the effective programs and the factors leading to that effectiveness?

At one time or another, we may have found ourselves in situations similar to the following scenarios. Our local governing board has just challenged the college president regarding the worth of our contract education program: How do we know companies are benefiting from this effort and what has the college gained from this program? Can we respond quickly to these questions?

As the managers of a contract education program, we just received a call from the state agency wanting to know how many students and employees our program served last year; types, sizes, and numbers of businesses served; and the dollars generated. Can we respond quickly and accurately?

A major employer with a strong presence in our state has just contacted us and requested that we submit a bid for training services at a site near our college. We know that they have worked with community colleges before and are very particular about the approaches used. Do we have any "inside track" communication mechanism for determining which colleges they have worked with and, more important, what approaches and pricing were successful?

If our answer was no to any of these questions, then it is time to either develop a management information system (MIS) for our program or improve our current system. In this era of scarce institutional resources, we need a system that can provide this kind of information quickly and easily. In this chapter, we present the rationale for such a system, depict an ideal information system, and describe a system currently in place in one state, California.

Framework for a Contract Education Management Information System

The system that is developed should be structured so that information is obtainable and not just data. One of the definitions of *information* in *Webster's New World Dictionary* (1986) is a "person or agency answering questions as a service to others," in contrast to *data,* which are a "collection of facts and figures" where the analyst must have knowledge to draw conclusions. The information retrieved should have relevance and purpose and should be timely, accessible, and empowering to the user (Drucker, 1989).

Typically, the contract education program manager will find that if the college MIS is used, the information received is incomplete for his or her needs. The college system is student-focused in that it provides data on the demographics of the students enrolled in the classes (for example, number of students, ethnicity, and gender) and the final grades received. No information is provided about the employer (for example, type and size of the business) or the size of the invoiced contract, nor is there a summary of past business and potential for future business with this employer, or tracking of any contributions that have come to the college as a result of the relationship with this employer.

In addition, contract education managers need financial tracking capabilities, much like small business operators. These program managers find that they are often a "school within a school." They need a system that enables them to generate payroll documents, accounts payable and receivables, or at least to notify the appropriate college office that such needs to be done.

The system should be able to evaluate the effectiveness of the training at a higher level than just customer satisfaction. This evaluation model should be multifaceted in that it measures the instructors' and program participants' performances. It is also desirable to measure the employees' performance in relationship to improved work performance and productivity. In order to evaluate the improvement in work performance, a careful assessment has to be done, prior to the start of training, to determine which indicators to use and how improvement will be measured (Kirkpatrick, 1976). The information gathered at this step drives the course content as well as the measurement tools.

The information received from this type of evaluation not only helps the employer (customer) to justify training costs for current and future training programs but also enables the college manager to quantify the benefits of a contract education program to employers. The program manager should be able to answer the question "What difference did the training program make?" The ability to answer this question becomes a powerful proactive means by which to validate the contract education program.

The MIS of the local college should be standardized with systems used by other colleges in the state so that information can be collected that describes programs and their impact in an aggregate fashion. There is a growing awareness among state policymakers that customized training conducted by community colleges benefits both the communities and the individuals trained. Practitioners need to agree on a means of measuring successful implementation and, then, communicate the results to state policymakers (Jacobs, 1992).

Finally, contract education providers need to seriously consider the benefits of becoming part of an "expert network" that would enable them to access other professionals like themselves for information-sharing purposes. Contract education providers need to realize that they are in a competitive environment and are brokers regarding the latest trends and techniques in work force development. Expert networks represent a new dimension, an electronic societal and organizational dimension, that did not exist prior to the development of computer-aided communication (Peters, 1992). It is through the use of an expert network that contract education program managers can identify solutions, people, and resources for their work force development challenges similar to those described in the introductory scenarios of this chapter.

Outlook for the Role of Management Information Systems

An examination of exemplary business performers of the last two decades reveals that MISs are a key component of success. Computer networks that serve as an informational infrastructure and control system continue to play a major role in organizations worldwide. This extensive technology is being utilized by organizations large and small, in part resulting from advances in computer technology. Hardware and operating systems have been developed that allow office automation power that would have been unattainable as recently as a decade ago.

Commensurate with this technical sophistication, there has been an important shift in management methods. There is a strong movement that routinely subscribes to employee empowerment and a belief that workers, where appropriate, should contribute to and share in the organization's most basic functions as well as its mission. As part of this employee empowerment, workers need access to information within the organization in order to make the right decisions. The use of computer technology is fundamental in this new organizational approach.

It is essential that workers have tools at their disposal to maximally effect organizational productivity, competitiveness, and customer responsiveness. This approach is best expressed in the principle of information responsibility (Drucker, 1989). The people who are responsible for carrying out the actual work are, in fact, the best qualified to shape and carry forward their contributions to the organization's mission. Recognition of the individual as part of team dynamics is expressed by investment in personal development and by provision of appropriate tools and resources. It is in this manner that organizations become increasingly aware of themselves and the competition. The organizations will then know what business they are in, their key strengths, operational parameters, and informational measurement tools.

A Network Primer

When discussing an ideal MIS for any enterprise, it is helpful to first consider three broad categories of computer technology: applications, networks, and operating systems. Applications are programs that provide an interface to the user so that he or she can indirectly access and manipulate the computer's resources. Examples of these programs are the various word-processing, spreadsheet, and data base programs with which most people are familiar. We can think of an application as a vehicle to get us to a specific destination.

Simply put, networks are computers that are connected together and have some level of commonality so they can "talk" to one another. This talking is termed *protocol*. To extend this analogy, a network is like a road that connects one location to another. Protocols, then, are the rules of the road. Networks allow for two basic services: resource sharing (working in groups) and computer-mediated communication (communicating with a work group). Together, these services allow users to access remote devices and programs, as well as to participate in electronic mail, conferencing, and bulletin boards.

Operating systems constitute the set of instructions that the computer needs to operate itself and its various input and output devices. Operating systems may be thought of as the driver's manual for operating a particular vehicle.

The three categories above, when taken as a whole, allow the magic to happen. This integration of systems comprises the basic binding technology essential to doing business today. Indeed, in a setting of global competitiveness, wherein the high-technology, customer-focused, quality-control-oriented players are the survivors, information capability is imperative.

Of the two basic services provided by networks, resource sharing is considered the most vital to business. Resource sharing was the impetus behind the development of distributed computer networks (Quarterman, 1990). The benefits are many: Equipment and users can be geographically dispersed, costs can be shared across the enterprise, management layers can often be reduced, aggregate information can be compounded from detailed data, and incremental expansion and redundancy are made easier. However, the irony is that it can take considerable resources to partake of resource sharing!

Computer networks can be cantankerous beasts. They require clever design and thoughtful management by skilled technicians if their benefits are to be realized. Moreover, network operating systems, dedicated linkages, host equipment, and routing devices are not cheap. Applications that are meant for network implementations have to be programmed differently from those intended for isolated computers.

Even so, we believe that some degree of computer networking is essential to conducting business in the next decade. Community colleges need to realize the value and efficiency of being part of an expert network. The power of leveraging information to improve business decisions will make a major difference in the marketplace. Just the ability to take different views of the information, looking at all of it or using the application to filter it, lends vitality and immediacy to the information. This ability is often lacking when the same data are presented by traditional upward reporting protocols. Viewing the output of a data base search that has limited its scope parameters is very different from reading a "sanitized" financial report. All levels of management have access to the original data without someone summarizing or interpreting the data. Access to information has become, and rightly so, more of a security than a political issue. Decision makers and policymakers are now better able to base their actions in reality with a view to where the business is actually being carried out.

Reality and a Contract Education Management Information System Model

What then is the reality for most contract education providers within a public higher education system? It is a time of unrest in higher education. Nowhere is this more true than in contract education. Contract education is one of the pivotal points around which the paradigm of public education delivery is shifting. The training requirements of America's work force are demanding alternative methods of curriculum development, class scheduling and location, cost accounting, and recruiting. Community colleges are becoming market-driven.

Contrast this characterization with the traditional structure, wherein colleges are reimbursed on the basis of course offerings that have been sanctioned through bureaucratic channels. We stress this difference not to pass judgment on either structure but rather to explain why current MISs are more accommodating of the traditional delivery modalities associated with credit curricula and students. Because the main sources of revenue are outside of the contract education enterprise, the support systems are outside too. This situation is well and good for the general computing needs of the college, but it often leaves the contract education practitioner out of the information-processing activities.

Our goal is to arm contract education practitioners with the basic knowledge needed to articulate their needs in a manner that is understandable to MIS personnel. This will allow them to enlist sufficient assistance and support from their local or central MIS department to carry through an initiative to the appropriate decision-making bodies. The intent is to help the contract education practitioners who are relatively naive about computer networks and data bases grasp the essential elements necessary to build a case for the establishment of a contract education MIS of some type in their organization.

Ideally, this system would be integrated with the existing campus MIS. However, most college systems are currently large mainframe-based installations. Unfortunately, these systems, though powerful, are often problematic. Maintenance and redesign are expensive. They may be already operating at capacity and are often remotely located in the data-processing department.

Fortunately, a starter system for contract education does not require the sophistication of the system needed by the rest of the campus. Also, there are many possible levels of networking. Most contract education offices have at least one or two computer workstations at their disposal. These may be connected to each other. These may be connected with other computers on-campus, which, in turn, may be connected to other computers off-campus, and so on. While isolated computers are useful, integrated computer networks are the ideal. However, where resources do not permit the implementation of a full-blown enterprisewide network, it is quite feasible utilizing certain application development techniques and simplified telecommunication technology to achieve, in effect, the same thing.

There are basically two ways of networking over a wide geographical area. One is resource-intensive and the other is relatively easy to attain. The first scenario involves connecting computers via a wide area network (WAN). A WAN requires dedicated cabling links between nodes, which allow for high-speed transmission across a wide band of frequencies. Special operating systems and hardware must be used for this type of configuration to function. This type of network technology, though powerful, is beyond the reach of all but the most successful contract education offices. Where it is feasible, however, remote users can take advantage of true interactive applications on shared resources. Data bases that comply with this design are termed *on-line real-time systems,* or *batch update systems.* Apart from the obvious advantage of continually freshened data, their main advantage is ease of management due to resource sharing. All users, no matter what their locations, are using the same standardized system to access a single related data base. A familiar example of this type of network is an airline reservations information system. The data base is constantly being updated by remote users throughout the entire network.

The second scenario is an alternative strategy that gets a contract education office into the game for considerably less money. Although, strictly speaking, these are not true networks, these "virtual" (in computerese, that means pretend) systems can take different forms. These solutions are variously referred to as *distributed data collection networks, file-transfer-capable bulletin boards,* and, most commonly, *sneaker nets.* Implemented with a wide range of sophistication, they are not real time or interactive, but they are affordable. Basically, these systems utilize a central data base flanked by several other nearly identical data base structures that are distributed to the practitioners in the field. The central data base is then updated periodically via floppy disk, file transfer from a bulletin board, or dial-in modem ports. Thus, the field-based systems are essentially distributed data collection points, while the central system is a global report generator.

California's Contract Education Data Inventory System

This latter type of system has been utilized by the California Community Colleges Economic Development Network (ED>Net). In 1991, ED>Net began the development of an MIS to undertake a statewide inventory of contract education activity. The name of the system is the Contract Education Data Inventory System (CEDIS). The purpose of CEDIS is to provide information to the local manager, as well as aggregate information on regional and state levels, about the scope and breadth of contract education programs. Working closely with a statewide committee of contract education practitioners, staff at ED>Net developed CEDIS. In 1992–1993, the system was pilot-tested by 13 colleges. Based on the results of the pilot, CEDIS was revised and distributed to all 107 community colleges in California in Fall 1993. Figure 4.1 depicts the basic architecture used to implement CEDIS.

The approach described here was used for several reasons. One is affordability. Another is the unlikely prospect of bringing an entire education system up to a networking technology level sufficient to use an on-line system, such as connecting computers via a WAN. Moreover, a relatively low-technology approach is often better accepted by casual users. Toward this end, a system was devised that would be easy to learn and use. It would provide some local site management capability for those who had no automated systems in place. Efforts were made to keep the system simple, limiting recorded elements to the bare essentials.

Generally, system design starts with an examination of the work processes of the information unit (in this case, the contract education office). Once the dynamics are understood, a sketch of the essential data elements can be drawn. This leads eventually to a data structure to contain the elements, a set of relations among the elements, assignment to appropriate program objects, and so on—in short, a detailed system design.

The initial design for CEDIS is contract-driven. The system tracks at the level of the employer and not the individual trainee. When field-based users first enter the CEDIS system, they are automatically routed to an area of the program that requires them to supply information about their contract education programs. This is how each distributed system is initialized, so that the central system can keep Provider A's data separate from Providers B's. Keep in mind that all distributed applications in a sneaker net are identical in all respects except for the information they contain. In other words, the same bottle can hold any kind of wine.

A contract is entered under the organization that holds the contract. The

Figure 4.1. CEDIS Architecture Flowchart

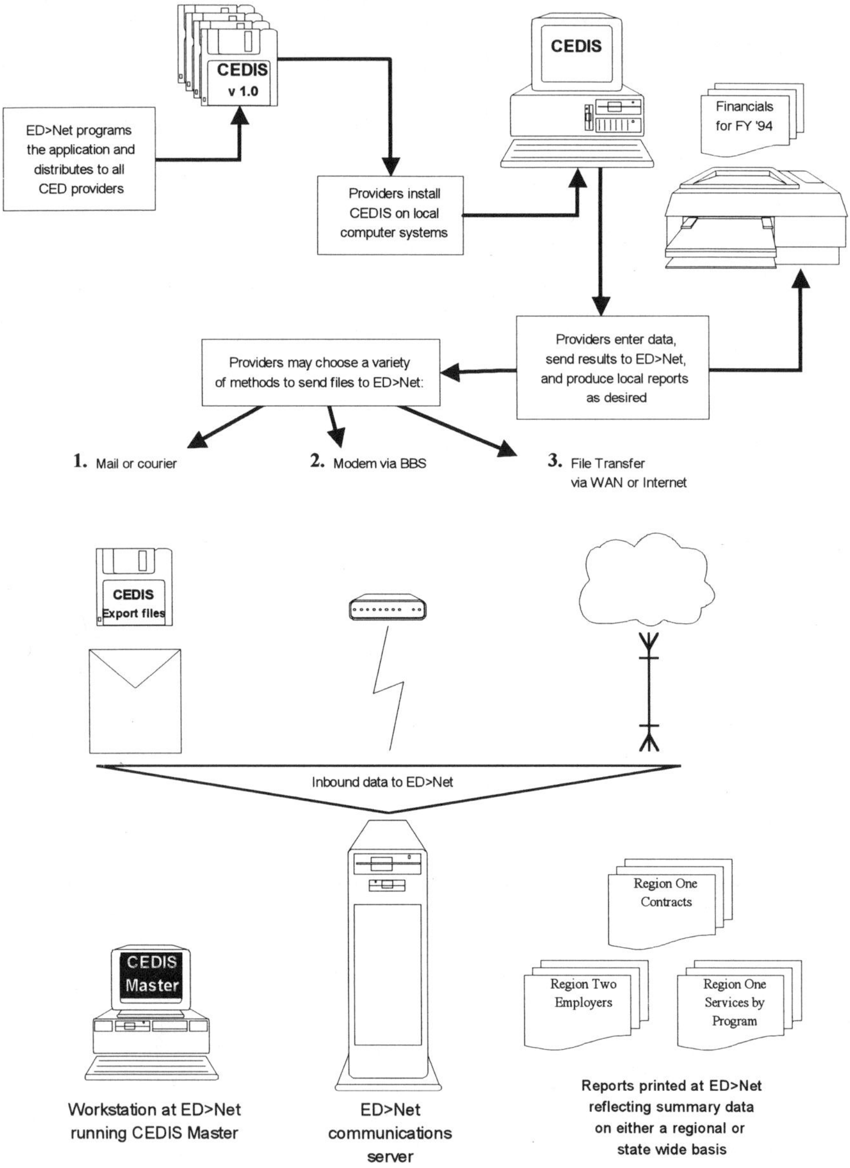

CEDIS
v 1.0

CEDIS

Financials
for FY '94

ED>Net programs
the application and
distributes to all
CED providers

Providers install
CEDIS on local
computer systems

Providers enter data,
send results to ED>Net,
and produce local reports
as desired

Providers may choose a variety
of methods to send files to ED>Net:

1. Mail or courier   **2.** Modem via BBS   **3.** File Transfer
via WAN or Internet

CEDIS
Export files

Inbound data to ED>Net

CEDIS
Master

Region One
Contracts

Region Two
Employers

Region One
Services by
Program

Workstation at ED>Net
running CEDIS Master

ED>Net
communications
server

Reports printed at ED>Net
reflecting summary data
on either a regional or
state wide basis

system automatically assigns a unique identifier (contract identification number) to each contract, so cross-references can be made to other data bases as needed. Users are constrained to a limited number of choices for certain data elements. This ensures accuracy and standardization of measurement. It also speeds data entry.

Once the program has been initialized, data regarding a contract are input. Windows are utilized for ease of entering data, editing, deleting, and so on. To add a new contract, the appropriate window is highlighted. This brings up a blank contract information screen. The fields are blank and get filled in by the user. Similar procedures are followed to edit or delete a record.

A completed contract information screen is illustrated in Figure 4.2. In the completed contract information dialogue box is all the necessary information about this contract between one of the California community colleges and the California Highway Patrol. A closer look at the specific contract elements shows that groupings may occur based on Standard Industrial Classification codes, public versus private agency, company size, and other relevant attributes. Each element provides a window into adding, editing, or deleting records in each of its associated data bases, to which it is linked.

Once the contract is entered, it takes its place in the contract browse window. This window is actually a powerful program object that can be searched, filtered, and otherwise manipulated by the user. In the contract browse win-

Figure 4.2. Completed Contract Information Screen

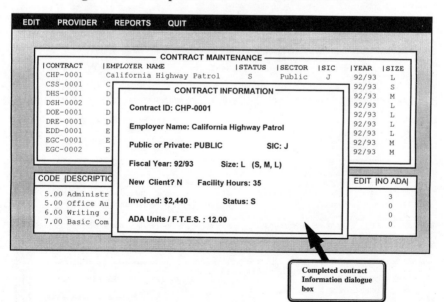

dow is a list of contracts by this college as well as the program and services delivered for each contract.

Synchronized with the contract windows are the program information windows. These windows are where the user provides the information about specific programs and services, which are then linked to a specific contract. In CEDIS, the user is guided through this process in a manner that builds a standardized program code. This enables measurement of activities within any particular program. A list of codes has been developed that enables all courses and services to be classified.

Once all of the data for the collection period have been entered, the user invokes a utility pull-down menu for export to ED>Net. This produces a compressed file of all data structures needed by the central system. Having accomplished this, the user can then use one of the three methods illustrated in Figure 4.1. The user could use mail or courier, modem via a bulletin board system (BBS), or file transfer protocol on Internet. Upon receipt, the file is imported into the central system so that global reports may then be produced based on the entire user base.

The heart of the system is shown in Figure 4.3, the CEDIS master program. There are three windows on this screen, enabling a triple browse: provider data base browse, associated contracts or contractor browse, and associated program browse. By highlighting elements in any one of these three windows, the user can more fully explore the information or data behind these elements.

Figure 4.3. CEDIS Master Program

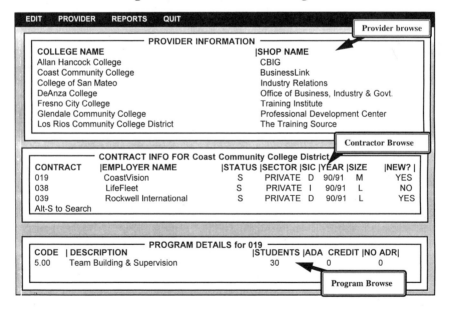

An additional important feature of this system is the query module. The query module enables the user to explore the data base and generate reports as needed utilizing the data in a useful format. For example, if the user wants the report to contain only information on contract amounts greater than $5,000 in the fiscal year 1993–94, he or she can construct the appropriate filter, which is then passed to the program to build the report accordingly. This interface thus alleviates the user from the task of having to construct a relatively arcane computer instruction such as inv_amount > "5,000" and fis_yr = "9394". This has been simplified considerably to illustrate a point because the actual program code required to achieve this functionality is more than one hundred lines long.

Once filters have been developed for reports in prior sessions, they can be saved for future use. This is very helpful if one has to prepare reports for different audiences utilizing the same information. In this manner, the same report could be utilized for senior management, boards of trustees, faculty groups, and so on. Each group receiving the report can decide for themselves the level of detail they require of the entire information set.

This system is but one state's initial step toward building an information network for contract education providers and others in the arena of community college work force development. The development and adoption of this system have been at a relatively modest cost. The capability of this system would be enhanced considerably if there were actual dedicated links among the users.

The development and adoption of technology continue to progress. The CEDIS model presented here has been revised and updated. To enhance its effectiveness as a local site management tool, financial tracking has been added. Also, it appears that ED>Net and the California community colleges will be linked with Internet. Internet is a network of computer networks. More than ten million people use this worldwide web of eleven thousand interconnected computer networks to exchange electronic mail, transfer computer files, search data bases, and electronically communicate in real time with other users.

As the California community colleges link up to Internet, we are enthusiastic about the expansion possibilities that will be provided for CEDIS, the expert networks that contract education providers will be able to access, and the overall improvements in communications. We look forward to being able to electronically communicate with contract education providers nationwide as technology becomes more widely utilized.

References

Drucker, P. F. *The New Realities.* New York: HarperCollins, 1989.

Jacobs, J. *Customized Training: A Necessary Priority for Community Colleges.* Warren, Mich.: Macomb Community College, 1992.

Kirkpatrick, D. L. "Evaluation of Training." In R. Craig (ed.), *Training and Development Handbook: A Guide to Human Resource Development.* (2nd ed.) New York: McGraw-Hill, 1976.

Peters, T. *Liberation Management.* New York: Knopf, 1992.
Quarterman, J. S. *The Matrix: Computer Networks and Conferencing Systems Worldwide.* Maynard, Mass.: Digital Equipment, 1990.
Webster's New World Dictionary. (2nd ed.) New York: Simon & Schuster, 1986.

MAUREEN H. RAMER is director of economic development and contract education for the California Community College Economic Development Network (ED>Net) in Seal Beach, California.

MIKE SNOWDEN is director of information systems for the California Community College Economic Development Network (ED>Net) in Clovis, California.

In order for a community to be successful in recruiting businesses,
a variety of partners must be involved. A true collaborative effort
must be seen by potential business clients.

Recruitment Practices: A Community Partnership

Julie Bender, Larry D. Carter

In this chapter, we outline the activities and partnerships that are typically a part of a community's effort to attract new business and industry. A key factor in the recruitment process is community partnerships. A community must convince prospective business clients that relocation to a new area, which is an expensive venture for any company, is worth the costs. Competition among the regions, states, and even localities is fierce and, therefore, demands that all of the resources available through community partnerships be brought to bear in the recruitment process.

It is important for the local community college to be a player in the recruitment effort. This involvement of the college can range from a minority partnership in the process to leadership in contacting recruiters and relocating clients.

The primary role of the community college is typically to facilitate and broker training. In some cases, this is a major incentive in a company's evaluation of a community's attractiveness. In other cases, issues such as quality of life and incentives offered by the local community are more important than the training issue. The community college must, therefore, have a balanced view of its role in the community partnerships that are vital to success when recruiting business and industry.

Partners in the Recruitment Process

Both the direct and the indirect roles that community colleges play in recruiting new business and industry are important. Community college officials need to understand how they can support economic development councils, cities

NEW DIRECTIONS FOR COMMUNITY COLLEGES, no. 85, Spring 1994   © Jossey-Bass Publishers

and counties, chambers of commerce, local elementary and secondary school districts, and other agencies in attracting new business and industry to their locale.

Economic Development Council. If a local county or municipality has an economic development council or corporation, that body is typically the lead player in recruiting, soliciting, offering incentives, and following through on efforts to relocate business and industry to the region. A strong economic development council can focus the efforts of the other entities involved in order to maximize the community's image and effectiveness in attracting businesses.

Local economic development councils can be stand-alone entities funded solely from private sources. In some cases, the economic development body is a private-public partnership; in other cases, it is an extension of the local chamber of commerce or a consortium of chambers of commerce; in still others, it is an actual arm of the city or county government. The involvement of the community college in the economic development council is essential if education and training needs are evidenced by clients. The college should be represented on the economic development board and should be able to broker or respond to education or training requests as they arise.

In most cases, the board of directors of the economic development council is a combination of a private-public partnership and, as such, has the best opportunity to coordinate packages that may be offered to potential clients to facilitate relocation.

Cities and Counties. Cities and counties are typically key elements in economic development for their areas. Where large sums of money are not available for direct incentives to potential clients, cities and counties can offer a variety of noncash incentives, including up-front agreements with potential clients with respect to various infrastructures such as roads, water, sewer systems, and utilities. Some clients are interested in a reduction of initial relocation expenses, which can be offset by a long-term commitment to the city or county. This commitment is evidenced by trade-offs that produce future jobs and tax income for the local municipality in exchange for up-front assistance. Thus, the city or county is in a strategic position to provide various infrastructure items in exchange for long-term revenues from the client that relocates.

Because time is money and relocation is a lengthy process, cities and counties can also offer incentives such as reduced turnaround time in permits and special assistance in interpreting and meeting codes and ordinances that might otherwise be unduly restrictive on the client's ability to relocate.

Chamber of Commerce. The local chamber of commerce traditionally has a strong role in the economic development of the community. Very often its role is to serve as an ombudsman for small businesses in the local community in relation to city and county policies, zone codes, and so on. Many chambers of commerce have evolved into the economic development arena as the local representatives for recruiting large businesses and industry. This new role generally requires a different set of procedures for dealing extensively with businesses outside the community. The advent of economic development bodies separate from the chamber of commerce was in part a result of this need. Although this role is generally filled by the economic development council or corporation, the chamber of commerce still has a strong role to play in the partnership.

The chamber of commerce still represents the "flavor" of its community. This flavor may take the form of quality of life, business friendliness by the city or county, and the general tax structure of the state and the city. The chamber has the ability to promote the community in conjunction with the economic development council. The chamber is seen as an accurate reflection of how business is done in that community, and thus, in terms of integrity, the chamber affects how the community is viewed by the client.

School Districts. When chief executive officers (CEOs) of companies who are facing business relocation look for a barometer of quality of life in the community, one of the first indicators they examine is the local school system. Company executives who make relocation decisions are very much concerned about whether their employees' children will have quality schools to attend.

The school districts are often seen to reflect the quality of the work force available in hiring new employees. Some companies look at percentage of high school graduates, percentage of those who continued their education, as well as the percentage of college graduates as indicators of the availability and quality of the labor force. Strong school systems generally have strong community support. These communities are generally good places to live in that community support is multidirectional, encompassing other activities in the community.

Postsecondary Education. The community college should be in a prime position to serve as a broker for a variety of training and education needs. The needs of clients from business and industry may exceed the capability of the local community college. However, that does not preclude the community college from facilitating the role of the university, vocational school, or private trainers that can be of assistance.

Very often industries prefer one-stop shopping and like to deal with one point of contact. If the community college positions itself in this manner, it can still assess the need for training, develop the customized training package for the particular business, and then assist in making the appropriate contacts that can deliver the necessary services. In this way, the community college maintains its visibility and contact with the industry and performs the function of facilitator.

Another advantage of the facilitator role is that the evaluation of the training program is accomplished by one entity and the community college is placed in the additional role of evaluator of training programs. These programs should be evaluated in terms of how well they met the needs identified during assessment.

Other Agencies. The broker model described in the previous section can be used to access other agencies that are part of the training network. The community college as deliverer should be familiar with the federal and state programs that are available in support of training needs in business and industry. The proper agency to be used is generally determined by the size and nature of the business or industry, the products they produce, and the type of labor force they employ.

The Job Training Partnership Act (JTPA), implemented through local employment and training offices, provides training funds for specific industries if the individuals trained are in at least one of the disadvantaged or dislocated worker categories in which JTPA programs specialize. These programs vary from summer youth programs, basic skills programs, and retraining for new occupations to career education programs for dislocated workers. In addition, some JTPA funds flow through state coordinating agencies, which provide direct grants to community colleges for certain kinds of training programs.

The U.S. Department of Labor is also in the business of training and is a possible source of funds for such activities. Labor unions are also in the training business, largely through apprenticeships. A state's department of labor is typically a good contact for information regarding union programs and U.S. Department of Labor funding.

For companies that have fewer than five hundred employees, the U.S. Small Business Administration provides direct training to small businesses as well as grants for agencies that are interested in assisting such businesses. In most states, the Small Business Administration funds small business development centers that exist for the sole purpose of providing counseling and start-up business assistance for small businesses. In addition to such initial assistance, many chambers of commerce, cities, and community colleges provide continuing assistance for small businesses.

Recruiting the Client

Business recruitment is a highly competitive activity across the United States. Hundreds of communities are competing for a limited number of back-office locations, new manufacturing plants, and new distribution facilities. Communities, to be competitive, must take a team approach to economic development.

To be an effective member of this team, community colleges and vocational schools should view their role with companies as long-term and market-driven. Recruiting a company is only the first step in the process of developing a training partnership with the employer. The goal should be to establish a long-term relationship that results in bottom-line cost and time savings to the employer. The training provider must design programs with the user in mind rather than try to make the user's needs conform to existing institutional programs.

This section answers three questions for the training provider: (1) "How can I most effectively package and market my training programs to business and industry?" (2) "What are the typical steps in recruiting a new company to the community?" (3) "What role do incentives, particularly training incentives, play in a company's site selection decision?"

Marketing. Communities vary in their economic development efforts. Some economic development groups are parts of chambers of commerce, others are government agencies, and still others are public-private partnerships. In some states, the state organization plays a lead role in economic development, whereas in other states, a support role. Whatever the configuration of a community's program, the training provider should approach economic development with the following directives in mind:

Be a member of the network. To be a part of the economic development network, the plan and the players must be known. The state, regional, and local economic development agencies should have strategic plans. The training provider's and economic development agency's plans should reinforce each other. It is also necessary to know how the area's economic development organizations are structured and who the key players are in these organizations.

Be a part of the local partnership. Every community should have a business recruitment team that is coordinated by the local economic development agency. This team should involve the top business and government leadership in the community. As experts in industry training, community colleges and vocational schools should play an important role on this team. With the growing importance given to work force development issues by companies, participation by the community's training providers is essential.

Involve top institutional leadership in the program. The president of the community college or vocational school should be a member of this team. His or her involvement makes a statement to prospects and to the community that economic development is a top institutional priority.

Make the program a top priority. In addition to the president's involvement, a high-level staff person should be designated to serve as the college's representative to business on a day-to-day level. This person should be responsible for coordinating the training providers' services to industry. The college or school representative should be able to speak industry's "language" and, most important, be able to deliver services to clients.

Be ready to hit the ground running. To become part of the business recruitment team, the college or school representative should be trained in working with prospects and should have professional marketing materials and a strong presentation. The local economic development agency can provide "ambassador" training so that the college contacts are familiar with the community's overall presentation. The college or school should have a presentation to clients that answers these questions: "What customized training services can you deliver?" and "What is your track record?" (Incorporate success stories.) In preparing the materials and presentation, keep in mind that quality is as important as content in creating the right business image for the institution and for the community.

Steps in Recruiting. The process of recruiting a company to a community begins with lead generation and ends with the company establishing a facility in the local community. Here are the typical steps in business recruitment:

1. *Generate prospect leads.* Leads are generated through the economic development agency's business recruitment program. The goal of the program is to generate leads in businesses and industries that the community has targeted for their growth potential and fit with the region's assets.

The local economic development entity should focus its lead generation efforts on relationship marketing. Advertising, direct mail, and media relations should be used to create awareness of the community and to position it in the marketplace. Do not, however, rely on advertising to generate bona fide prospects. Instead, focus on the referral network. By and large, economic development prospects are generated through relationships. Referrals most commonly come from the development industry (real estate, construction, engineering, and architectural firms), professional service firms (law and accounting, primarily), the financial industry, and contacts in the companies. Relocating a company is a big decision. Decision makers start the process by talking to people they know.

2. *Qualify the prospect.* The job of the economic developer is to qualify the prospect. Careful screening of prospects is important so that the economic developer's time is spent on the right projects. On a very basic level, a potential client's responses to the following questions can help the developer identify legitimate projects: Type of contact (for example, consultant, manufacturer, distributor, provider of business services, real estate developer, real estate broker or agent)? Number of employees? Expansion or relocation? Possible or in progress? Headquarters or branch operation? Age of company? Type of information or services most helpful to company at this time (for example, site selection services, economic or demographic profile, housing and quality-of-life information, personal telephone call)?

Economic development staff typically sift through large numbers of inquiries to qualify an active prospect. To illustrate this point, the Metro Denver Network (a regional economic development organization) tracked prospect activity from January 1991 to July 1992. During that time, the network handled 664 inquiries for information. Of the 664 inquiries, 73 became active prospects.

3. *Make the initial contact.* Every active prospect should have an assigned account executive who coordinates all information to the client. The account executive serves as the single point of contact for the client and ensures that

the client is given consistent information. An assigned account executive is essential for delivering exceptional customer service to prospects. The quality of customer service can be as important as the community's other features in the client's site selection decision.

In initiating contact with the agency, the client may call on its own behalf or may use a contact in the community. Larger companies may use site selection consultants to represent them.

The initial package that is sent to the client should respond to the clients' request without a proliferation of unrequested material and should be received by the client as soon as possible. Demonstrating an ability to respond quickly may be as important as the actual contents of the package.

The initial package to the client should contain overall community information as well as background on customized training. The package information may cover available land and facilities, local business climate and labor supply, access to supplies and services, level of public services, transportation and distribution facilities, environmental issues, utility availability and cost, and well as training programs.

4. *Host the site visit.* Through follow-up with a client, the economic developer further qualifies the client. Once the developer establishes the project's legitimacy, the goal should be to get the client to visit the local area. A site visit is a must if the community is ultimately going to secure the project. The prospect's site selection team may consist of one or several people. In some cases, the company sends an advance person, who will plan a site visit for a larger team. Some companies send a real estate team (physical site issues), a human resources team (labor quality, cost, and supply), and a quality-of-life team (schools, housing, and cultural and recreational amenities).

Larger companies may have corporate real estate executives in charge of their site searches. Increasingly, companies are making the human resources director an important member of the site selection team.

The economic developer must determine who within the company will make the site selection recommendations and the decision. Knowing the decision maker's "hot buttons" is critical. The economic developer's job is to coordinate the community's business recruitment team and to work with the company in establishing a schedule of meetings and tours for the visit.

The community's business recruitment team should match executive levels and functions with the prospect's team. If the prospect's CEO visits the community, the community should reciprocate with CEO-level representatives.

During the client's first visit, a briefing should be conducted. The format can vary, but a menu-driven audiovisual presentation is an effective means of tailoring the information to meet the client's needs. The community's presentation must be tailored to the interests of the client. Nothing loses the client's attention faster than having to sit through a presentation of unwanted information. The presentation should provide an overall business introduction to the community. Using a computer menu, one can select sections on community history, quality of life, business statistics, or regional transportation, depending on the client's time and interest. Whatever the contents of the presentation, the economic developer must set the meeting agenda to maximize the value of the client's time in the community.

In addition to the briefing, the economic developer should arrange for other members of the economic development team to be present at the site visit meeting to answer the company's questions. The team should have a prepared agenda for the meeting and should be briefed ahead of time about the client by the economic developer.

After the briefing, clients visit with resource people in the community. Because the work force is an important issue, many clients want to visit with the human resources directors of local companies in addition to reviewing published information. In meeting with human resources directors, the clients often ask questions about labor availability and quality. The site visit team may also ask about the services provided by local community colleges and vocational schools. These meetings are often held without the economic developer and community college representatives in the room so that the candor of local companies is not impeded.

The local economic development team should strive to increase its closure rate with companies who make site visits. The closure rate is a good indicator of the effectiveness of the team in attracting companies to the community. For example, before the creation of the Metro Denver Network, the Denver metropolitan area's estimated closure rate on site visits was about one-third; that is, one-third of the companies who visited Denver selected the metropolitan area as a business location. After six years in existence, the network has increased its closure rate to about two-thirds, reflecting a tremendous improvement in community marketing.

5. *Follow up.* After the initial site visit, the economic developer should follow up with the client, delivering additional information and preparing for subsequent visits by the company. Again, the local response should be coordinated by the account executive.

Initial contact with the company is just the first step. Patience is a virtue in business recruitment. Site selectors may start with a long list of states and cities and cull the list by painstakingly evaluating potential sites in relation to company criteria. As site selectors focus on communities that meet their needs, communities may have to survive a first, a second, and even a third cut.

Companies may also refine site selection criteria as they obtain new information. By the end of the site selection process, the project definition may have completely changed. As projects evolve, business recruitment teams must demonstrate their flexibility and willingness to work with the prospect.

Projects may also be put on hold or delayed by the company. To be successful, business development requires sustained, consistent effort over a long period of time. Site selection decisions can take two or three years.

Ethical Considerations. Two ethical issues that often arise in business recruitment are confidentiality and negative selling. Policies on these issues should be clearly conveyed to all members of the economic development team before business recruitment begins.

All client information should be kept extremely confidential. Leaks about company plans or intentions can prevent any further consideration of the community and seriously damage the credibility of the local economic development program. To preserve client confidentiality, the economic developer normally assigns the prospect a code name or client number.

If a leak occurs, company management may be deluged by complaints from its employees who were unaware of relocation considerations and by calls from realtors and other salespeople. Sensitive information may be revealed to the company's competitors. This type of disruptive activity could cause the company to abandon its relocation plans altogether.

Another ethical issue is negative selling, that is, pointing out negatives of a competing community. While it is acceptable to use comparative data showing what one's own community has to offer compared with other cities, it is not okay to "knock the other guy." Let the clients draw their own conclusions about the competition. The economic development presentation should focus on the community's assets and how negative attributes are being addressed. To prevent negative selling, a code of ethics should be adopted by all parties involved in area marketing.

Incentives. Incentives are the most widely publicized and most misunderstood aspect of economic development. Project publicity often focuses on incentives, although there usually are many other factors in the site selection process that are more important.

In situations where two or more competitors are rated equally in relation to project criteria, incentives can be a tiebreaker in a deal. Their real significance, however, is usually not in relation to the project's bottom line because the dollar amounts are small compared to the total project cost. Incentives are often best used as a good-faith effort to show a community's commitment to a project. If a company is using incentives as its leading criteria in site selection, this may not be a project that the community should pursue.

Incentives should be used judiciously. Each project considered for incentives should be evaluated against a set of incentive criteria that makes sense for the community. Sample incentive criteria are as follows: (1) *Competition:* Is an incentive package necessary to be competitive with other potential locations for the business? (2) *Target industry:* Is the business being considered for an incentive package in a targeted industry? (3) *Creditworthiness of company:* What is the quality of the company that is seeking incentives? Is it well known regionally or nationally? Is it well established in the marketplace? Does it have a good credit history? (4) *Return on investment:* What is the anticipated return on investment to the city or region in terms of tax revenues and to the community in terms of jobs and payroll? (An economic impact model can be developed to gauge the return on investment.) (5) *Leverage:* Does the city's participation leverage incentive dollars from other sources such as state and county government?

In offering incentives to companies, consider the use of training assistance or infrastructure improvements. If the company later downsizes or relocates, the community still has the benefit of a trained work force, physical improvements to the site, or both.

Examples of Community Partnerships

How community colleges can assist in new business recruitment efforts is perhaps best decribed through illustrations of several community partnerships at Community College of Aurora, Central Piedmont Community College, and Redlands Community College.

Aurora Briefing Center. One example of the outgrowth of a strong community partnership is the Aurora Briefing Center, located on the campus of the Community College of Aurora in east Denver, Colorado. Although the site was orignally designed as the boardroom for the college, located next to the President's Office, the community partnership that evolved among the college, the city of Aurora, the Aurora Chamber of Commerce, and the Aurora Economic Development Council spawned the idea of converting the boardroom to a briefing center for profiling the community to potential relocation clients.

The concept centered around a leading edge audiovisual presentation, complete with a laser disk video, a mouse-controlled menu, and computer-based programming. The college agreed to allow the Aurora Economic Development Council to have the highest priority in scheduling the room for clients making site visits to Aurora. Thus, the boardroom became the Aurora Briefing Center. The college has second priority in scheduling any activities other than those involving an Economic Development Council client.

The city of Aurora and the Aurora Economic Development Council each contributed matching funds to the upgrading of the briefing center. In addition, Humana Hospital and Comprecare contributed to the project. In-kind donations were given by M. A. Mortenson, a contractor; International Design; and the Development/Design Consortium. The audiovisual package was furnished at a discounted rate by Cimarron International, a local media design company.

When a prospective client visits Aurora, the first stop is the Aurora Briefing Center. This is where the audiovisual showcasing of Aurora is presented. It provides maximum opportunity for the customized training office at the college to visit with a client about potential training needs, if required.

The briefing center further provides a one-stop shopping package for the client and allows flexibility in profiling Aurora through a menu-driven audiovisual production. The briefing center also serves as a physical reminder to clients of the true partnership that exists among the Aurora Economic Development Council, the city, and the college.

Central Piedmont Community College. The state of North Carolina utilizes an economic development strategy that relies heavily on training incentives to attract new industry. For example, the state allocates resources to train employees of new and expanding industries through a program administered by the state's community college system. The program works as follows. The General Assembly appropriates funds each year for the new-industry program. Administratively, the Department of Community Colleges receives the funds and reallocates them to colleges based on individual project needs. These dollars are expended not only to attract new businesses to North Carolina but also to serve the needs of companies going through significant expansions.

Each community college that has potential projects in its service area works locally with organizations that are interested in economic development to make business prospects aware of the training services offered by the college. Without fail, one of the economic development players is the local chamber of commerce. Typically, an economic development team is formed. Team members include, at a minimum, the college's new industry director and one or more individuals from the chamber of commerce's economic development group. This team interacts with the potential client to make the company aware of the training incentive package available to relocating firms.

As an example of how this partnership between the community college and the local chamber of commerce works, the industry relocation team of the Charlotte Chamber of Commerce recruited First Data Corporation to Charlotte. The company develops and sells complete software systems for health care organizations. Part of the incentive for the move was the promise that Central Piedmont Community College would provide extensive training for First Data in order to enable its work force to reach productive skill levels. At present, Central Piedmont Community College has delivered multiple classes to almost every First Data employee. Courses range from Introduction to Computer Skills to Complex System Integration. There is no charge to the company for this training.

What are the benefits to each partner in this approach? For the community college, the answer is obvious. Economic development is part of the college's mission, and establishment of ties with new industry leads to long-term relationships in which the companies continually look to the college to meet their training and education needs. For the chamber of commerce, there is access to a service that benefits its members. For the company, the benefits include a comprehensive training package that includes in-depth training needs analysis, customized screening and evaluation, curriculum development, customized course delivery, and training facilities and equipment. And, for the community at large, the partnership yields business and industry growth, thus more jobs.

Redlands Community College. Leadership programming and training as a new format of community education guided through a local community college is not a totally new idea or community services activity. Far from it!

However, it can present a "win-win" enhancement of experiences for all concerned. Harlacher and Gollattscheck (1992) cited the building of communities as the new rallying point for U.S. community colleges. The term *community* is defined as not only a region to be served but also a climate to be created.

Redlands Community College in El Reno, in Canadian County, Oklahoma, believes that leadership development has a direct tie to the quality of life available in a community and thus has a strong relationship to economic development. It is necessary to have a strong community to assist existing and new businesses with access to services and to provide a high quality of life to their employees. Redlands has gone even further in its climate creation by establishing and operating Leadership Canadian County, a leadership development and networking program.

Forerunners of this county leadership program were team-taught leadership courses that were part of a model consortium effort that included the Kellogg Foundation, the Phi Theta Kappa academic honor society, and pilot community colleges nationwide. Based on this recognition of need for local community-based networking, Leadership Canadian County evolved.

Just as business operations and educational institutions study change and impact, Leadership Canadian County surveys various quality-of-life issues. In order to ensure a blend of the actual and the potential, the leadership project elicits responses, discussion, and recommendations on each topic. Thus, infrastructure or police and fire services not only are site-witnessed and discussed by participants but also follow-up responses are given to various city and county groups and councils studying the topic. This reality-based but free-thinking design entails review in focused, concerned, quality-enhancement formats where shared ideas and pooled resources can be tested for future application.

By making Leadership Canadian County an informed, committed, and involved program, Redlands Community College has given the county today and in the year 2000 and beyond a foundation to improve its economic climate and its standard of living for citizens of all ages. People with reality-based ideas and talents can create enthusiasm, desire, and the determination to propel themselves and their communities forward, thus allowing Canadian County to meet the challenges of the future in a shared, planned, and empowered profile.

Canadian County includes seven separate communities, with an overall population approaching one hundred thousand people. No specialized grant or local college budget has been created, and no release time personnel have been assigned to this program, but a climate-building commitment to enhance Redlands Community College by enhancement of the publics served has been made based on a belief in people. Redlands Community College agrees with the Commission on the Future of Community Colleges (1988) that "the most challenging task before our college and all community colleges in the future is the building and rebuilding of our communities to the ultimate end of building learning communities that empower people to participate in continuous individual and community renewal" (Larry S. DeVane, personal communication, April 1993).

References

Commission on the Future of Community Colleges. *Building Communities: A Vision for a New Century.* Washington, D.C.: American Association of Community and Junior Colleges, 1988. 58 pp. (ED 293 578)

Harlacher, E. L., and Gollattscheck, J. F. "Building Learning Communities." *Community College Review*, 1992, *20*, 29–35.

JULIE BENDER *is president of the Aurora Economic Development Council, Aurora, Colorado, and past chair of the Metro Denver Network.*

LARRY D. CARTER *is president of the Community College of Aurora and vice president of the Aurora Economic Development Council.*

As a result of the need of U.S. industry to become more competitive with foreign markets, issues surrounding workplace literacy have emerged. In many instances, our current work force is illiterate in relationship to the new environment of the workplace.

Beyond Work Force Literacy: The Hidden Opportunities of Environmental Literacy

Bob Cumming

What Really Happened to Put Us in This Mess?

Over the past ten years, a massive change has occurred in the American workplace, one that has redefined the nature of work as well as the type of workers needed. Essentially, three major factors can be seen as integral parts of the change and responsible for the United States' slow start toward becoming globally competitive. The primary force driving this transformation was, and remains, advancing technology (U.S. Department of Education, 1992).

If we had conducted a survey of business and industry ten years ago and asked the question "Are literacy issues a major concern in productivity?" the answer would have probably been no. Prior to the introduction of the computer to the manufacturing arena, the majority of workers had a sufficient level of basic skills required to measure, assemble, and produce products. However, once the computer and its related technologies became permanent fixtures in industries across the nation and around the world, what formerly sufficed as basic skills were no longer enough. Today's workers are required to make complex decisions, operate sophisticated numerically controlled production equipment, and understand new and intricate concepts such as participative management, statistical process control, and just-in-time production.

The second factor affecting U.S. competitiveness is training. When the first of the new technologies were introduced, there was a glut of workers on the market with appropriate skills. Employers were able to select the top candidates for these new positions rather than promote from within, thus little investment was made to provide training for the existing work force. As a result, both the employer and the employee lost and the competitive edge slipped further from America's grasp.

On a collision course with these trends was the third factor, changes in the pool of future workers. While technology continued to increase the demands for higher basic skills, the number of available qualified workers had been exhausted. Seventy-five percent of the people who will constitute the American work force in the year 2000 are adults today (Chisman, 1989). Employers are reaching out to less qualified workers to develop entry-level work forces (U.S. Department of Education, 1992).

So now we know what happened. But what are the solutions to this problem and how can we capitalize tomorrow on the investments we must make today?

Environmental Literacy Versus Basic Skills Literacy

Today, literacy in the workplace has taken on a new perspective. We no longer can limit literacy to reading, writing, and the ability to perform mathematical calculations. Workplace literacy encompasses much more, as highlighted in *Workplace Basics: The Skills Employers Want* (Carnevale, Gainer, and Meltzer, 1988). Seven specific skill areas were identified as critical to today's work force. In addition to reading and writing and mathematics skills, learning to learn, problem solving, self-esteem, teamwork, and organizational effectiveness are now included. This is a prescription for a well-rounded worker who has acquired a number of discrete skills and who has the capability to acquire more sophisticated skills when necessary (Carnevale, Gainer, and Meltzer, 1988).

Another way of looking at this "new-wave literacy" was presented to me several years ago as environmental literacy, which is the ability to function within a specific environment (Davis, 1989). For example, the first time we travel to a new city, we may not know street names or locations of hotels and services. For a short period, we are illiterate within this new environment. Taking this same theory to the workplace, we can see that as statistical process control is introduced, the employee must learn how to plot charts, compute mathematical equations, and report significant findings. Until trained and comfortable within this new environment, the employee cannot function in a totally literate manner.

Those who have experience in dealing with many different companies and organizations have found that the majority of services requested revolve around basic skills such as mathematical computation or language comprehension and communication. Since many employers are only familiar with educational achievement as measured by grade levels, they ask that the instructional program increase the grade level of the employee by a specific amount. However, most experienced workplace instructors now regard grade levels as irrelevant for workplace programs. The preferred approach is to develop competencies that relate directly to the tasks required in a specific job. Therefore, the measurement is based on competence attainment or, in other words, increases in the employees' environmental literacy.

Conducting Environmental Literacy Audits

Over the past few years, I have had the opportunity to work on three separate projects in which environmental literacy audits were conducted. These audits were designed to identify the specific competencies of a job that, when attained, would provide the employee with the capacity to be both flexible (able to change jobs within the same organization) and mobile (able to move between organizations). The audits met the employer's needs of determining company-specific competencies validated by effective employees and reducing turnover while maintaining a stable, effective, well-trained work force in order to compete effectively.

Based on the aforementioned definition of environmental literacy, eight individual categories were surveyed: job-specific skills, basic skills, preemployment skills, work maturity skills, communication skills, learning to learn, organizational effectiveness, and teamwork skills. Two instruments were designed to conduct the audit. The first was a questionnaire, which was used for multiple-level interviewing to obtain input from managers, supervisors, and employees. The instrument used open-ended questions to, first, solicit initially direct responses to the formal items and then provide the opportunity to interviewees for informal discussion and follow-up questions or response elaborations. The questionnaire moved, in order, from specific to general, from key words to roles, from soft data to hard data, and from formal language to informal language (see Exhibit 6.1).

The second instrument was an informal observation checklist of organizational environment and behavior (see Exhibit 6.2). Using this instrument, the interviewer toured the worksite and observed multiple characteristics that affected the workplace environment.

Once the audits were complete and the data compiled, a list of appropriate skills areas was developed. The information derived from literacy audits can assist the employer in the development of accurate job descriptions and employee evaluations, provide the employee with a sound foundation on which to build skills in specific areas, and furnish educators with competencies that can be used in designing curricula. Examples of skill areas identified by a literacy audit of a medical front office include (1) knows terms connected with insurance documents, (2) categorizes calls by content, person, and action needed, (3) uses proper identification when answering the telephone, and (4) estimates accurately required waiting time for patients.

Exhibit 6.1. Interview Schedule

1. Is there a written job description for this occupation?
   Is there a copy available for use in this literacy audit?
2. What are the five major skills of an effective employee?
3. What are the five most important reasoning/thinking skills of an effective employee?
4. What are the five most important interpersonal relationship skills an effective employee uses with fellow workers and supervisors?
5. What are five specific job skills that are most important to be an effective employee?
6. What are the five learning or training skills that are most important to be an effective employee?
7. Does the organization use forms to document tasks and activities?
   If yes, what are the five written communications skills that are most important to be an effective employee?
8. Does the organization use a formal performance appraisal system?
   If yes, is the occupation under audit included in the system?
   How often are formal performance appraisals conducted?
   (Annually_____ Semiannually_____ Quarterly_____ Other_____)
9. Does the organization use company manuals?
   If yes, how are they used?
       Orientation
       Policies and procedures
       Work directions
       Other
10. Does the company have an organizational chart?
    Is a copy available for use in this literacy audit process?
11. Does the company have a formal quality program?
    If yes, what is the employees' role in the program?
12. Rules of the organization/business
    Are they formal (for example, orientation manual) (_____) or informal (_____)?
    What purpose do the rules serve?
        Safety_____ Conformity_____ Other_____
    What assumptions about the relationship of employees to the business do the rules suggest?
    Do the rules suggest management or employee attitudes/behaviors?
    Does the business have rules for dress/appearance?
        Are they generally followed (observation)?
        What purposes do they serve?
        Safety_____ Conformity_____ Other_____
        What attitudes do they reveal?
            Toward employees?
            Toward customers?
        Do the rules communicate the kinds of behavior the business values?

Exhibit 6.1. (continued)

13. In your own words, what is the company's main purpose?
14. What key words or phrases are used by employees regarding the company's purpose?
15. What are the three most important roles of an effective employee?
16. How does an effective employee fit into the overall purpose of the company?
17. How does this specific job relate to getting other company positions?
18. Do you have any comments or questions you would like to add?

Source: Davis Consulting, 1991.

Exhibit 6.2. Informal Behavioral Observation Checklist

1. Where is the location of the work activity in relation to the rest of the organization?
   Central_____ Peripheral_____ Other_____
2. Surroundings
   Is the work area accessible (disabled) and easy to reach?
   Is the work area secured? Are there locked doors? Fences?
   No Trespassing signs? Visitor Report to Office signs?
   Building guards? What purposes do they serve?
   Do the security precautions suggest any underlying assumptions about the relationship between business and employees?
3. Environment
   What are the architectural features of the building(s)?
   What kind of activities does it seem to encourage?
   What purposes does the architecture seem designed to serve?
   What kinds of special facilities does it have?
   What kinds of objects are visible?
      Pictures?_____ Signs?_____ What about?_____
      Banners/flags?_____ Trophies?_____
      Mottoes? (List/quote)_____
   Who are the people pictured in the halls, on the bulletin boards, and named in plaques in the business?
   For what reasons are they honored?
   What are the common characteristics of these employees?
   On the basis of these models, can you make any inferences about the values of the organizational culture?

Exhibit 6.2. *(continued)*

What kinds of attitudes do these items portray?
  Rules/Regulations
  Human activities (celebrations, informal activities, and so on)
  What kinds of activities does the business seem to honor in such objects?
  Does the environment suggest any inferences about the kinds of activities the business values most?
How is the facility arranged internally?
  Offices_____ Cubicles_____ Other_____
What assumptions about status do the furniture and arrangement suggest?
What is the interior decoration/appearance like?
  Clean/messy?   Colorful/dull?
  Open/closed?   Comfortable?
What lines of communication does the facility seem to encourage?
What kinds of behaviors do the facilities seem to encourage?
What kinds of equipment are available for employees to do their work? (Up-to-date and so on?)

4. Organizational Activities
What kinds of rites and rituals are performed at regular intervals within the institution?
What seem to be the purposes of these rites and rituals?
What organizational values do they reflect?
What kinds of symbols do they involve?
What roles do employees play in their performance?
What role do managers play?
Does the community at large take any part?
What cultural beliefs do the rites and rituals encode and transmit to the employee?

5. Interviewing/Interaction Issues
Who poses most of the questions in the room?
Who does most of the talking?
Do employees listen attentively to their fellow employees?
What kinds of activities do the employees spend most of their time performing?
What habits or skills do these activities develop or reinforce?
What inferences would you make about the information and the skills the culture values most?
What kinds of models of behavior does the business provide?
How do employees behave?
How do employees speak?
What characteristics do they have in common?
In what ways do they differ?

6. Additional Notes

Source: Davis Consulting, 1991.

Identifying the Organization's Needs

When meeting with the company for the first time, the education provider must keep in mind that the problem, whatever it may be, has probably been ignored for some time. But now the company needs a solution yesterday and wants the training to begin tomorrow so as to have a trained work force by next Monday. Unfortunately, quality workplace programs cannot be delivered on such a short time line. Careful consideration must be given to all phases during the development, delivery, and evaluation of any program, and there must be a total "buy in" by all parties within the organization affected by the project. Without this buy in, the education provider will continually be battling with management pushing for shorter time lines, supervisors refusing to release their employees for training because of work schedules, union officials balking at the assessment and testing of employees, and employees showing little or no interest because they fail to see the relevance of the training to their jobs. For this reason, the development of a project planning team should be the first order of business for the second meeting with the company.

The planning team should consist of upper management (including human resources), supervisors, union representatives, select employees, and the education provider (including the curriculum developer). A comfortable group of about eight to ten individuals will work nicely. The purpose of the planning team is to oversee the entire project and deliver technical assistance to the education provider. The team will make decisions regarding curriculum, delivery schedules, employees to be served, evaluation methods, and, most important, the desired project outcomes.

The first task of the planning team is to identify the training needs. Again, the education provider should use caution if presented with a needs statement that has been developed prior to the creation of the planning team. If this is the case, key direct questions should be asked by the provider. For example, what method was used to identify the needs? Who was involved in identifying the needs? What types of measurable data exist that confirm the needs? If these questions cannot be answered to the satisfaction of the provider, a formal needs analysis should be conducted. None of the parties will benefit from a program that fails to increase employee performance and job satisfaction. If it is necessary for the provider to conduct a formal needs analysis, several issues should be considered. First, and probably most important, the planning team should play an integral part in designing the analysis format. After all, it is their business operations and employees that will be analyzed.

Let us assume that the perceived problem involves basic skills issues. In conducting the needs analysis, the education provider must first identify the job tasks, including the basic skills competencies, required to perform a specific job effectively. Through simultaneous observations and interviews of competent workers, critical job tasks can be studied to determine the context in which they are performed and the thinking process used by workers to apply literacy skills to task performance (Philippi, 1991). Some of the major steps in conducting a needs analysis include the following:

1. Structured interviews with management, supervisors, union officials, and employees to determine their perspectives on the perceived problem
2. Tour of the facility with special attention to the job area or production process that appears to be affected by the perceived problem
3. Review of job descriptions for critical task positions
4. Review of pertinent written materials, including manuals, signage, production forms, company memos, and employee handbooks
5. Review of any mathematical computations that must be performed by the employees and to what extent or frequency these computations are involved in the job tasks
6. Identification of the communication skills required to perform job tasks, including interdepartmental, cross-departmental, and external customer relations
7. Assessment of the importance of problem solving, critical thinking, and teamwork skills involved in performing job tasks

Needs analysis is a specialized field in its own right. It cannot be assumed that basic skills instructors necessarily have the expertise to perform needs analyses. Thus, the individual who is assigned this task should be the same individual who later develops the curriculum and has experience in conducting a needs analysis within a business setting, identifying basic skills criteria and their application to specific job tasks, working with culturally and educationally diverse populations, and developing human resources.

Once completed, the data generated by the needs analysis should be reviewed by the education provider. These data will become the foundation for any services provided to the organization and should be presented to the planning team in an easy-to-read format. It is recommended that the report include the following components: executive summary, report objectives, research methodology, problem definition, what needs to be done to solve the problem, who needs training, expected outcomes, overall recommendations, and evaluation of program effectiveness.

Once the planning team has had the opportunity to review and discuss the results of the needs analysis, the decision on how to approach the problem is the next task. This is where clear and achievable project goals are developed. These goals should be realistic in nature and address only the needs identified by the analysis. Any attempt to go beyond the identified needs not only can open the process to new, unidentified problems but also may cause the project to fail due to its inability to handle new issues. The next step is to develop a project time line that provides a target date for each goal and performance indicators to demonstrate that the goals have been achieved.

Selecting the Correct Delivery Methodology

Several issues must be addressed in order to determine the appropriate program delivery method. The first step is to identify the individuals who will participate in the training. Given that the needs analysis identified the tasks required to perform one specific job, it can be assumed that the target population will involve individuals within that job category, although it is entirely possible that not all of those individuals will require training. In order to determine the actual program participants, an assessment of current skills in relationship to job requirements must be conducted.

Because of the shortcomings of most commercial standardized tests—in particular, these tests do not adequately measure the basic skills required on the job—experts recommend that job-specific assessments be developed to determine employee needs (Longnion, 1991). To further complicate the process, many employers request the use of standardized tests since they provide numerical values such as grade levels, which many employers believe are universal definitions of skill levels. Workplace experts agree that grade levels have nothing to do with how skills transfer to the job (moreover, there are potential legal problems when standardized tests are used in the workplace). In order to effectively measure the current skills of the potential program participants, competency-based assessment instruments must be developed. Unfortunately, many education providers, new to the world of workplace education, feel inadequate in developing job-specific assessment instruments, even though there are numerous resources available both in the current literature and through other workplace learning professionals. As a result, it has become clear to these providers that professional development for faculty and staff is critical to the successful delivery of workplace programs.

Competency-based assessment requires predetermined standards of performance in defined areas (Longnion, 1991). The most effective instruments include a series of questions, problems, or exercises directly related to the job tasks. For example, if the job requires mathematical computations of a specific nature, such as calculating percentages and converting the percentages to decimal equivalents, the assessment instrument should include several exercises of that kind. Once completed by the participant, the instructor can evaluate the results and determine the proficiency level as well as the specific areas that need improvement. If the apparent need requires use of a competency-based reading assessment, the cloze procedure using job-specific text may be appropriate (*cloze* is derived from *closure*, meaning "to complete by encompassing"). This kind of test requires participants to form mental closures around missing pieces of information by using grammar and meaning clues from text—literally filling in the blanks (Philippi, 1991). A participant's ability to replace the missing words is an indicator of his or her level of understanding and comprehension. Other instruments can also be developed by using specific reading passages from job-related materials in conjunction with questions, or by having job-specific materials read aloud and asking the readers to restate in their own words the meaning of the materials. In the construction of any competency-based assessment instrument, the content of the instrument must reflect the findings of the task analysis and relate to the objectives of the customized curriculum.

Once the population of learners has been identified, specific instructional methodologies can be reviewed and an appropriate delivery method selected. During this process, several issues must be considered. For example, when working with a large population of individuals, an on-site classroom approach may be the most effective in meeting specific training time lines. However, when working with participants who are relatively small in number, such as fifteen to twenty, and who are split into two or more work shifts, computer-based instruction may be the most effective. Another consideration arises if the company has several different locations with no easily accessible central point for training. Many companies will not accept proposals that require their employees to travel to the training site. In these cases, a distance learning approach may be the answer.

As computer and software manufacturers present new products to the educational market, distance learning via computer technology has become more viable. For example, a customized curriculum package could be developed using one of the many "authoring" software programs currently available. Once the program is loaded onto a file server, the company for which the curriculum was developed has direct access available for any of their appropriate computer workstations through the use of a modem. This method enables a college to transport a variety of curricula to several companies all at the same time from a central location. An instructor need only monitor the progress of each of the distance learners and communicate with them by way of a bulletin board system. In addition, the instructor could schedule on-site visitations with the individual learners as needed. This approach could very well define one of the many new classrooms of the future.

In each of these cases, the experienced provider understands that not only is the curriculum content different from that used in the campus classroom but the delivery may or may not be led by an instructor. These two issues have fostered many heated discussions within the ranks of academia. Some faculty welcome the new technology and approach the possibilities for change with enthusiasm, while others remain bound to the textbook and classroom. Workplace education has brought to the forefront a variety of expanding opportunities for educators. For example, a new population of students who would probably never enroll in a traditional program now have the opportunity to continue their education with the target of increasing their job security by becoming more effective employees. Furthermore, the expanding technologies of distance learning, interactive video and video disk programs, and full-motion video supplied to the desk-top computer via fiber optics are changing the ways in which educational programs can be accessed by the learner.

One of the most recent advances in computer-based learning is the integration of authoring software and basic skills programs for the adult learner. Many educational software vendors have promoted their computer-based basic skills programs as effective tools in the workplace. This claim may be valid if learners are primarily interested in improving their basic skills to achieve general equivalency diplomas. However, as discussed earlier, true workplace learning must incorporate competency-based instruction that is directly related to specific job tasks. One vendor, realizing the need to relate the basics to the workplace, has effectively combined an authoring software package with the company's basic skills product. The authoring software allows an instructor to develop a competency-based workplace curriculum that interacts with the basic skills program as needed by the learners. Now learners can receive workplace instruction and improve their job-related basic skills at the same time.

Customizing the Curriculum for the Workplace

As the movement toward providing workplace learning programs continues to grow, so too does the need for qualified curriculum developers. Many education providers are finding that relatively few of their current faculty have experience in curriculum development. This dearth of experience is not surprising since many of the credit classes offered utilize one or more textbooks each from which a course outline or syllabus is constructed and the delivery of instruction is lecture-based. With a shortage of experienced curriculum developers, education providers are discovering that prior to delivering workplace programs, professional development for the faculty is a necessity. Instructors with previous work experience in the private sector may find it easier to make the transition from the classroom to the workplace and therefore to center their instruction on learner needs rather than on what they believe should be taught.

In workplace learning programs, the curricula are determined by needs analyses and participant assessments. From there, performance-based, functional context curricula are developed. The terms *performance-based* and *functional context* are relatively new with the emergence of workplace programs. Performance-based refers to the learners' mastery of those tasks that have been designated essential for successful performance on the job (Carnevale, Gainer, and Meltzer, 1988). Functional context refers to the use of job-related materials and concepts as the basis for training. Properly designed, the curriculum will eliminate the gap between what the learners know and what they need to know to perform their jobs effectively.

One of the major areas where functional context curricula are used is workplace English as a Second Language (ESL), which is rapidly becoming a significant training need in a wide array of industries. Its growth is fueled by the increasing numbers of non-native English-speaking immigrants who are filling the ranks of the employed from manufacturing to service industries. The key focus of workplace ESL, also commonly referred to as vocational ESL, is to develop listening and speaking, reading, writing, problem solving, critical thinking, and world-of-work skills by integrating specific language functions such as clarifying, following directions, and questioning and requesting strategies within the context of a job- or industry-specific curriculum.

Using the functional context approach to curriculum development, greater emphasis is placed on teaching communication functions needed at work as well as on teaching the specific vocabulary and language structures needed within the workplace context. Individuals from different departments and with different job titles can participate in the training at the same time by supplying specific terms from their worlds of work, such as names of tools, machinery, processes, and concepts. In this approach, employees generate their own workplace-specific contextual environment, and the curriculum teaches them to maneuver within it, for example, to ask for directions to the first step in a process, or to seek clarification or information about operating a particular piece of equipment (see Exhibit 6.3).

The most effective workplace learning or literacy curriculum incorporates techniques for building functional language skills along with a focus on teaching the specific language that is found in the environment or context of the workplace. As the curriculum is developed, the provider must determine how learner performance will be measured. Since most workplace programs are short in duration, and management is looking for increased performance and the bottom line, the learners' performance becomes a quality issue. There is a fundamental difference between the views of student progress in the classroom and the expectations of learner performance in the workplace. In the classroom, it is widely accepted that some students will receive grades of A or B, the majority will receive C's, and the low achievers will receive D's or F's. However, in the workplace, anything less than increased performance is unacceptable. This difference rests on the identity of the "customer." In workplace programs, the company is the customer, and the customer evaluates the provider on the quality of instruction through the increased performance of the employee.

Throughout the development of the curriculum, the education provider should continually meet with the planning team for several reasons. First, the planning team is made up of experts in the field. They may not know how to develop a curriculum, but they can offer valuable advice regarding content and areas of importance that should be included in the program. Second, the greater the extent to which the planning team is involved in the development process, the greater the buy in by management, union officials, and employees. The feeling of ownership by the planning team can facilitate all aspects of the project. Without this key element, the provider's time will be consumed by one operational problem after another.

Exhibit 6.3. Workplace Language Skills and Vocational English as a Second Language Training

Purpose: The purpose of this lesson is to teach the language functions of opening a conversation and gathering information. Some reference is made to the workplace context through the integration of specific terms, including electronics as well as names of actual supervisors and employees.

Examples of Starting Conversations and Gathering Information
With people you already know (informal)
1. Hi Joe! I need some information about _____. Could you help me?
2. Kathy, I wonder if you could help me with this?
3. Hello Lupe. I need to get some information about _____.
4. Hi Adriana, do you have a few minutes?
5. Nena, I need some help with this. Is this a good time for you?

With people you don't know (formal)
1. Excuse me, my name is _____ and I work in Electronics. I need some information about _____.
2. Hello, my name is _____. I wonder if you could help me?
3. Excuse me, my name is _____ and I'm from Disposables. I need to get some information about _____.
4. Excuse me, I'm _____ and I work for Kathy Smith. Could you help me find out about _____?
5. Hello, my name is _____. I work in Electronics and I'm trying to get some information on _____. Is this a good time for you?

Examples of Conversational Practice Items for Students
Openings: Can I ask you a few questions?
Asking for information: I need to know _____.
Clarifying and confirming: I'm sorry, I'm not sure I know that.
Closing: Thanks for your time. I really appreciate it.

Example of Practice Writing Activity
1. Question: _____
   Answer: Sure, what questions did you have?
2. Question: _____
   Answer: No, but I could meet with you at 2:00.
3. Question: _____
   Answer: Well, specifically, my job is to repair the 9000 models.
4. Question: _____
   Answer: For more information, you could try asking the supervisor in Disposables.
5. Question: _____
   Answer: Yes, some examples of that product line are the Model 7000 and Model 8000.

Source: San Diego Community College District, Workplace Learning Resource Center, 1991.

Evaluating Workplace Learning Programs

Evaluation of workplace programs is an ongoing process, similar to what is called "continuous process improvement" in the manufacturing industry. Evaluation consists of several different components, all of which generate data that will ultimately be used in the final report to the planning team. Providers must continually be aware that performance is the basis on which the program will be judged. The evaluation process is not a component that can be addressed at the end of the program. It must be a continuous strand, measuring quality and performance throughout the project. The evaluation process is formative in the sense that it is continuous, allowing for adjustment of plans, reallocation of resources, and other management decisions. The process is also summative in that it measures the effectiveness of the program in meeting the goals established by the planning team. An effective evaluation process includes the following elements:

Analysis of how the program meets the project goals. Throughout the project, the evaluator should determine if the implementation process is meeting the established project goals. If there is a significant difference between what was planned and what is occurring, steps should be taken to adjust the process.

Pre- and posttesting of all participants. The instruments designed for this process should include job-specific tasks. The process is ideal for the provider to measure the effective learning that has taken place during the instruction. In addition, the data become performance indicators, which the provider can use to validate the quality of the training program.

Criterion-referenced testing during instruction. The instruments designed are administered throughout the instructional program. With a preset criterion, usually expressed as a percentage of items correct or a percentage of objectives mastered, the results will indicate the participants' degree of mastery of tasks as identified in the performance objectives.

Structured interviews. Suitable with individuals or small groups, these interviews are designed to record the perceptions of participants, supervisors, and managers regarding the goals of the workplace program, the type of activities that should be included, and how they would know when a participant had mastered the objectives (Philippi, 1991). These interviews are part of the buy-in process and add to the feeling of ownership by the organization.

Classroom observations. This process helps the evaluator determine the effectiveness of instructor training and the value of specific instructional activities in order to draw conclusions regarding planned versus actual outcomes.

Participant surveys. These surveys are designed to obtain the participants' reasons for taking the program and to determine if the program is meeting the participants' needs. This process may provide the evaluator with different perspectives on the effectiveness and value of the training since the data reflect the participants' points of view.

Supervisor surveys. These surveys provide a basis for determining whether the workplace program resulted in improved job performance. Typically, these surveys are conducted both during training and approximately six months after training.

Implementation of an evaluation component requires appropriate planning by both the education provider and the company served. It is important to look at the implications and impact that the evaluation process has on the business, the provider, and, most important, the program participants (Longnion, 1991). The following areas should be addressed in the final report to the planning team: executive summary, program mission and goals, instructional process used, program participants, participant experiences and outcomes, preliminary evaluation of program effectiveness, and recommendations for additional training and services.

Unexpected Outcomes from Workplace Learning Programs

It is erroneous to think that once the training has been completed and the final report presented, the results of the project will only be seen in relationship to employee performance. There can be many unexpected and positive outcomes from workplace programs, some more subtle than others. For example, as a result of the planning and development process, both management and employees should have a clearer perspective on the organization's goals and future direction. Possibly for the first time, employees have seen that management does care about performance and quality and is willing to support employee-training programs. This realization helps build the employees' self-esteem and, therefore, reduces barriers to future training. Management, on the other hand, may realize the importance of investing in their work force. Through quality training based on a functional context approach, training time can be reduced by providing instruction that is meaningful to the employees, thus enabling them to experience a direct transfer of the environmental literacy skills they are learning to the workplace tasks they perform (Philippi, 1991). As employees become more productive, their mobility through the organization is enhanced and their value to the organization is increased.

There are also meaningful outcomes that can be traced to the needs analysis. Through identification of specific job tasks and the performance levels required to be effective, performance criteria can be developed and used to create an effective and legal employee evaluation. This information can also be used to create or update job descriptions in a manner that accurately reflects the requirements and skill levels needed for specific jobs.

Finally, the analysis may also identify the need to modify instruction manuals so that they can be used effectively. Unfortunately, most manuals are written at a level much higher than the reading ability of the average employee.

This may be due in part to the writers' inability to adjust their writing skills to the comprehension levels of the users. This discrepancy is most commonly evidenced in computer manuals. Many companies have found that by rewriting these documents, the employees' effectiveness can be increased without jeopardizing the process that is being explained.

Conclusion

The United States is in the tenuous position of wanting to remain a world economic giant but lacking a work force that can compete in foreign markets. For years, employers were reluctant to provide training to their employees for fear that once trained the employees would seek higher-paying jobs. Employees, on the other hand, became comfortable within protected union environments and approached training with a "maybe tomorrow" attitude. Today, however, many things have changed to bring these two, sometimes very opposing, groups together as one in their mutual battle for survival. We have learned that today's technology moves rapidly from one computer chip to another, and in its wake systems, processes, and jobs are affected.

Education providers must embrace these changes as opportunities to provide professional development for their staffs, design new and advanced educational methodologies and delivery systems, and, most important, provide customized training to a work force that must move into the twenty-first century confident of its ability to produce quality services and products.

References

Carnevale, A., Gainer, L. J., and Meltzer, A. S. *Workplace Basics: The Skills Employers Want.* Washington, D.C.: Government Printing Office, 1988.

Chisman, F. P. *Jump-Start: The Federal Role in Adult Literacy.* Southport, Conn.: Southport Institute for Policy Analysis, 1989. 47 pp. (ED 302 675)

Davis, D. S. *Workplace Literacy: Reading the Workplace.* Los Alamitos, Calif.: Davis Consulting, 1991.

Longnion, B. *Designing and Implementing Workforce Literacy: Programs in Partnership with Business and Industry.* Houston: North Harris Montgomery Community College District, Workforce Literacy Consortium, 1991.

Philippi, J. W. *Literacy at Work: The Workbook for Program Developers.* New York: Simon & Schuster, 1991.

San Diego Community College District. *Workplace Language Skills/VESL Training.* San Diego Community College District: Workplace Learning Resource Center, 1991.

U.S. Department of Education. *Workplace Literacy: Reshaping the American Workforce.* Washington, D.C.: Government Printing Office, 1992.

BOB CUMMING is director of economic development for the Workplace Learning Resources Initiative, California Community College Economic Development Network (ED>Net). He has been involved in workplace learning and assessment for the past fifteen years.

Training for trade must become a community college priority in preparing the U.S. work force for the increased global market of the twenty-first century. Community colleges across our nation can serve as an effective, training-for-trade delivery system.

Training for Trade:
A Partnership Strategy

Jack N. Wismer

75 percent of the market for U.S. goods lies beyond our American shores. Every $1 billion in U.S. exports generates about 25,000 new jobs.
                              —U.S. Department of Commerce

The United States will continue to be challenged by the market and work force demands of a global economy for the twenty-first century. It will take *vision, partnership,* and *persistence* for American companies to be successful competitors in the international marketplace.

Peter Drucker has been quoted as saying that there are two kinds of employers: those who understand the necessity of an international economy and those who understand unemployment. Fortunately, we are living in a time when business, industry, and education understand the critical need facing America for a skilled, trained, and educated work force. The time is ripe for American community colleges to become more proactive and make a commitment to the economic development initiatives that will stimulate community growth—especially international education and training-for-trade programs.

The American Association of Community Colleges, as part of its mission, supports increased curriculum emphasis on international and intercultural education. In its strategic report *Building Communities: A Vision for a New Century*, the Commission on the Future of Community Colleges (1988, p. 32) stated that "the goal should be to increase international awareness . . . through lectures, business seminars, and, when appropriate, international exchanges."

NEW DIRECTIONS FOR COMMUNITY COLLEGES, no. 85, Spring 1994   © Jossey-Bass Publishers

We have a responsibility to develop global awareness and work force skills among our students and business community. "To meet the needs of commerce and industry for a more sophisticated and globally competitive workforce, American business is again turning to community colleges" (Fifield, Foster, Hamm, and Lee, 1990, p. 15).

Training for Trade: Community College Role

Why should community colleges provide international trade education and training? Today, global competition impacts almost every business or industry through the international market of services and products. Students and business employees must develop the necessary skills to compete in a world marketplace.

Community colleges, by their mission, have a responsibility to serve their communities and prepare the work force for the twenty-first century. A key role of every community college is to serve area citizens and businesses—our customers, constituents, and taxpayers.

Global competitiveness often triggers corporate restructuring, downsizing, and a focusing on continuous quality-improvement efforts, as well as heightened efforts to globalize companies and increase exporting of products. American companies are now recognizing that to succeed tomorrow, they must succeed in a global economy. International trade is an excellent opportunity for economic growth and job creation.

To meet the competitive challenges of a global economy, American community colleges can better serve business and industry by promoting international trade awareness and providing the training needed to create a world-class work force. Community colleges continue to demonstrate a track record of customer-responsiveness in delivering quality training services to business and industry. Katsinas and Lacey (1989, pp. 13–14) pointed out that American businesses are looking more to community colleges as an effective training delivery system because they are already in place to provide quality education and training programs and services to meet the changing economic needs.

Equally important, community colleges have a responsibility to focus on increasing international trade education skills and thus to prepare a skilled work force for businesses to compete in a global economy. Community colleges must take a leadership role in providing international education opportunities and promoting training-for-trade programs. Training for trade focuses on three applications by providing (1) international trade training to employees of businesses and students who desire to gain export or import knowledge and skills; (2) technical training assistance by working in partnership with government, business, and other education resources to export American products and services; and (3) educational opportunities to students, citizens, and businesses to learn about international languages, customs, and cultures. We, as community college educators, are faced with an exciting challenge and opportunity to help our communities and businesses prepare the work force for a changing global marketplace.

Building Partnerships: Strategies for Success

While economic development is an integral part of the community college mission, the goal of establishing the necessary partnerships and strategies to maximize resources is critical to the success of international trade education programs. Building partnerships is key to implementing a successful training-for-trade program. Three strategies can help us achieve success:

Step 1: Building Support Within the College. The college should establish a cross-functional task force to develop a comprehensive plan that addresses all of the needs of international education and training at the college. The task force needs representation from college administration, corporate and community development, instruction, and student services.

An important task of a cross-functional college team is to develop shared goals that will benefit the college and the community. At Lake Michigan College, seven goals of this kind were identified: (1) to infuse a global perspective in all college courses for internationalizing the curriculum; (2) to expand international student services by focusing on the college's existing international student organization and developing additional support services; (3) to develop institutional and instructional enrichment materials that can be used as part of existing courses to stimulate an awareness of international trade; (4) to provide staff and student support, development, experiences, and exchange opportunities that enhance personal involvement and accomplishment and increase global awareness; (5) to implement an international business center to promote international trade awareness and provide training services for regional businesses in southwest Michigan; (6) to expand international education offerings in continuing education areas to better serve regional businesses and employees; and (7) to develop effective marketing strategies and resource materials to support the promotion of international trade awareness. Based on these seven goals, action plans were developed, including grant proposals to obtain funding sources as well as implementation models for internationalizing existing curricula and continuing education programs. The importance of the task force continues to foster cooperation and commitment to collegewide goals.

Step 2: Economic Development Partnerships. Community colleges across the nation are now recognizing the importance of forming alliances with businesses, government agencies, and local chambers of commerce to meet the challenges of a global marketplace. Successful training-for-trade programs involve partnerships among business and industry, education, and government. These partnerships are often referred to as economic development triangles (Pfahl, 1991).

By working in cooperation with government, business, and industry, community colleges can develop training-for-trade programs that develop competencies for students and business employees. These partnerships also help community colleges promote and fund programs that serve to strengthen local economic development. For example, the partnership for the International Business Center at Lake Michigan College works cooperatively with the U.S. Department of Commerce/District Office, Michigan International Office, Berrien County Economic Development, and Cornerstone Alliance (local chamber of commerce), which serve to cosponsor programs and provide trade assistance.

Step 3: Advisory Boards. To gain commitment for training-for-trade programs, community colleges can establish advisory boards from business and industry and economic development organizations. Advisory boards can provide valuable input into the development of training programs that increase the international skills of their employees. Members can also be extremely helpful in promoting training programs and serving as instructors for training modules.

At Lake Michigan College, the International Business Center Advisory Board meets quarterly to review programs and international trade education services and to provide suggestions for success. The board represents small export companies to Fortune 100 corporations and includes export managers, vice presidents, and presidents of companies.

To summarize, both internal and external partnerships are necessary to implement successful training-for-trade programs.

Delivering Effective Training Programs

The discussion below of some of the current community college training-for-trade programs highlights a variety of effective practices.

Central Piedmont Community College. In the 1980s, with a soaring U.S. trade deficit and a changing manufacturing base, Central Piedmont Community College recognized the importance of learning the basics of export trade to help North Carolina businesses survive. As a result, Central Piedmont has developed innovative training programs in response to the needs of business and industry.

Training-for-trade and continuing education courses in international trade and language training are providing the business community with quality, cost-effective training. The college currently offers a twenty-seven-hour noncredit program, including Letters of Credit, Principles and Documentation, International Marketing, and two transportation courses.

Waukesha County Technical College (WCTC). In 1984, WCTC, in Pewaukee, Wisconsin, launched an international trade program by offering both an associate's degree and continuing education training seminars. The target market for training workshops focuses on the needs of the technical and clerical staff of companies whose growth depends on expanding their markets to other countries.

Two of WCTC's most successful workshops, "Export Documentation and Payment Methods" and "Moving Cargo Internationally," provide practical hands-on training that is transferable to the workplace. In addition, WCTC has developed forty export training videotapes with learning guides, which have been marketed across the United States and Canada.

St. Louis Community College. Recognizing the importance of providing export assistance to the business community, St. Louis Community College collaborated with the U.S. Department of Commerce, World Trade Club, and Missouri District Export Council to assist small- and medium-size businesses that want to export products or are interested in expanding export markets.

Export readiness clinics were developed to assist new-to-export companies by assessing export potential, matching products with export markets, and conducting training workshops on marketing, sales, documentation, and financing. The clinics were funded jointly by the U.S. Department of Education (Title VI-B, Business and International Education Program) and St. Louis Community College. The workshops feature practical, how-to sessions with experienced practitioners in international business. Upon completion of the clinics, an export business plan is developed for each participant's firm.

North Seattle Community College. The International Trade Institute was founded in 1987 to fill the gap in international education and thereby respond to growing market pressure from the international business community to provide practical training for global trade. The institute is a resource center that provides professional training services in international trade.

With input from an advisory board, a thirty-credit certificate in international trade program was designed for business owners, employees, and entrepreneurs. The certificate courses include Fundamentals of Export, International Trade Geography, Practical International Marketing, Cultural Imperatives in International Business, and International Transportation. In 1988, more than eight hundred Seattle area residents participated in classes and training workshops. The institute also provides contractual training services tailored to individual business needs.

Portland Community College. Small businesses contribute significantly to Oregon's economy. The Small Business International Trade Program was established in January 1986 to provide comprehensive training services that assist small businesses in world trade. It represents an effective partnership at Portland Community College with the U.S. Small Business Administration, Oregon Small Business Development Center Network, and Oregon Economic Development Department.

As a result of this partnership, several training programs have been established to help small businesses become active in international trade:

First Friday: an introductory seminar for businesses considering international trade

Trade Tuesday: a series of international trade classes helping small businesses enter export markets, expand existing international trade, and train key employees

International Incubator: an intensive four-month program of class work and on-site counseling benefiting companies ready to export into international markets

Regional Trade Councils: a statewide network administered through the Small Business Development Center to build a coalition of private and public interests to focus on international trade development

International Small Business Exchange: a business-to-business exchange program created to foster international trade opportunities with countries throughout the world

Lake Michigan College. In 1990, the Corporate and Community Development Division conducted a survey that identified a minimum of 123 businesses engaged in international trade distribution. As mentioned earlier, the International Business Center was established to work in partnership with Cornerstone, Alliance Berrien County Economic Development, Michigan International Office, and the U.S. Department of Commerce to promote international trade. An advisory board of businesses and economic development agencies was formed to provide guidance to programs and services.

Funding awarded from the U.S. Department of Education (Title VI-B, Business and International Education Program) enabled Lake Michigan College to expand its International Business Center to focus on international education and export training programs. As a result, the center has implemented the following programs and services to benefit the business community:

Export Advantage: an international trade certificate program developed to increase knowledge and skills for employees about international business practices

Training for Trade Workshops: a series of practical, how-to workshops on doing business with Mexico, Japan, Germany, and other countries, providing business employees a focused approach to export markets

International Business Trade Survey: a follow-up survey designed to identify products, markets, and services

International Trade Resource Library: a collection of over 18 videotapes, 20 audiotapes, and 150 international trade reference resources to assist faculty, students, and the business community

Video Training: a series of self-paced, or workshop, video training modules designed to reinforce the how-to workshops and to increase the knowledge and skills of students and employees

College of DuPage. Skilled in training and responsive to the long-term business development needs of local companies, community colleges are strategically positioned to prepare businesses to export successfully. The International Trade Center is part of the Business and Professional Institute at the College of DuPage, providing training and technical assistance to small- and medium-size firms.

The goal of the trade center is to target businesses with export potential by providing training services. Its cost-recovery training programs and services supply resources not readily available elsewhere. The center's services include a trade information clearinghouse of guides to exporting and 130 country files, technical assistance in marketing products to key markets, trade lead identification and dissemination, and training-for-trade education workshops. One workshop, "How to Sell Overseas," is a series of ten evening sessions designed to develop international skills. The series is developed in partnership with the U.S. Department of Commerce, Small Business Administration, Illinois Department of Commerce, and College of DuPage. As an outcome of the workshop, the center's staff work with participants to develop an export marketing plan.

Middlesex Community College. In 1987, in response to a heightened and expanding interest in international trade opportunities by local business and industry, Middlesex Community College, in Massachusetts, conducted a comprehensive survey of area firms to ascertain the training needs and support services necessary to develop these opportunities. A direct outcome of the survey was the development of a variety of innovative initiatives, including international trade degree and certificate programs; short-term seminars on a variety of trade issues; faculty and student exchange programs with Russia, Hungary, South Africa, Japan, and the People's Republic of China; an active visiting scholars program; and a branch campus in the People's Republic of China.

In December 1992, Middlesex Community College opened the branch campus in China. This innovative program provides intensive, short-term, noncredit business courses for government officials and entrepreneurs. The program has been described by one faculty member as "Capitalism 101." These courses are very focused and utilize a "cookbook" approach stressing how to convert from a planned to a free-market system. Included in the course offerings are Macroeconomics, Financial Accounting, Finance, Marketing Strategies, and International Trade. Each course concludes with the awarding of a certificate.

All instruction is delivered in English and then translated by university-trained interpreters. All instructional materials, overheads, and handouts are bilingual. The faculty have found the delivery of instruction through interpreters to be more efficient than initially anticipated.

The courses have been provided in both Beijing and Jinan, with additional sites scheduled to open in Quingdao, Rizhao, Hebei, Shanghai, and Hainan

Island. The courses are offered on a fee-per-participant basis and have provided a significant and expanding revenue stream for the college.

Training Services and Resources

International training-for-trade programs may differ at community colleges in the kinds of programs and services offered; however, they focus on the common goal of providing quality education and training in promoting international trade. Access to training-for-trade resources is necessary to strengthen international trade programs. Community colleges can obtain computer software and videotapes and participate in professional international trade associations.

National Trade Data Bank (NTDB). NTDB is a one-stop resource for international trade and export data from fifteen U.S. federal government agencies. NTDB contains over one hundred thousand documents, including basic export documentation that is released monthly on CD-ROM at a reasonable cost. NTDB is a valuable resource tool for community colleges in their efforts to assist business and industry customers. For more information, contact the U.S. Department of Commerce at (202) 482-1986.

Company Readiness to Export (CORE). This computer program guides a company through a series of questions to determine commitment levels, products, and target markets. Based on responses to these questions, CORE provides an assessment of the readiness of a company to export in a global marketplace. For more information, contact Michigan State University International Business Center at (517) 353-4336.

National Association for Small Business International Trade Educators (NASBITE). This national association serves to improve global competitiveness through effective education and training. With an emphasis on how-to programs to promote international trade, NASBITE offers the following training benefits for members: specialized international education and training workshops and access to trade resources such as curricula, course outlines, and video materials. The annual conference gives community colleges the opportunity to share information on programs and resources. For further information, contact NASBITE at (503) 223-3896.

Looking to the Future

Threats to and opportunities in America's economic development are coming from more than one direction: technology change, work force demographics, and global competition that requires training and retraining. American community colleges must focus on preparing our students and business community for a global marketplace.

Training for trade is directly related to the community college mission. To achieve our goals as quality training and teaching colleges in America, community colleges must take a proactive role to serve adult learners, our customers and taxpayers, beyond traditional international study programs and focus on lifelong learning skills that improve employee productivity.

Joyce S. Tsunoda, chancellor for community colleges, University of Hawaii, in addressing the 1988 annual meeting of the National Council on Community Services and Continuing Education, emphasized the role of community colleges in international activities: "'Training for trade' is built on the thesis that the economic development of a nation depends on well-trained workers and that community colleges, with their traditional partnership with industry, with their emphasis on local economic development . . . can and ought to be in the forefront of the nation's response to meeting international trade competitiveness" (Tsunoda, 1989, p. 3). Training for trade must become a community college priority in preparing America's work force for the twenty-first century. Community colleges across our great nation can serve as an effective, training-for-trade delivery system.

References

Commission on the Future of Community Colleges. *Building Communities: A Vision for a New Century.* Washington, D.C.: American Association of Community and Junior Colleges, 1988. 58 pp. (ED 293 578)

Fifield, M. L., Foster, S. F., Hamm, R. and Lee, C. J. "Workers for the World: Occupational Programs in a Global Economy." *Community, Technical, and Junior College Journal,* 1990, *61* (1) 15–19.

Katsinas, S. G., and Lacey, V. A. *Community Colleges and Economic Development: Models of Institutional Effectiveness.* Washington, D.C.: American Association of Community and Junior Colleges, 1989. 97 pp. (ED 312 006)

Pfahl, N. L. "Using a Partnership Strategy to Establish a Trade Assistance Program." In L. Huhra and M. L. Fifield (eds.), *Training for Trade: Community College Programs to Promote Export.* Washington, D.C.: American Association of Community and Junior Colleges, 1991. 212 pp. (ED 330 422)

Tsunoda, J. S. "Reaching Out: The Role of Community Services and Continuing Education in International Education." *Community Services Catalyst,* 1989, *19* (1), 3–8.

JACK N. WISMER is vice president of corporate and community development at Lake Michigan College, Benton Harbor, Michigan.

By assessing the cultural climate of an organization as a first step, education providers can gather essential baseline information about an organization and hence provide a guide for more skills-specific assessment, curriculum development, delivery, and evaluation.

Environmental Workplace Assessment

Jacques Bernier, Nancy Jackson, David Moore

An environmental workplace assessment is not only a valuable tool in developing customized training but also a necessity if problems are to be identified and lasting changes realized. The purpose of the workplace environmental assessment process is (1) to gather data to assist in determining how employees in the organization view the assigned tasks and the environment in which those tasks are accomplished and (2) to analyze the data and the organization to enhance the development of the work force and the quality of the work environment.

The effectiveness of a customized training process depends on a carefully planned and customized assessment. To execute an environmental workplace assessment, the educator should consider the following six questions in the planning state: What process will yield best results training in the organization—group discussion or individual interviews? Who would be best to conduct or facilitate the assessment—company or college officials or some combination? How will the data be gathered—written surveys, group discussion, or a combination? How long will it take to complete the process? What is the extent of the assessment, and how many aspects will it measure and to what depth? How will the data be analyzed, summarized, presented, and utilized?

Several processes can be utilized to assess an organization. The size and nature of the organization determine what combination will work best. The group process and individual interview techniques are described here.

NEW DIRECTIONS FOR COMMUNITY COLLEGES, no. 85, Spring 1994 © Jossey-Bass Publishers

Group Process

The advantage of the group process is that it enables the educator to collect a great deal of information in a short period of time and maximizes the amount of participation. It is quite straightforward. The object is to gather data from a cross section of an organization in a group setting. If the organization is small enough, the ideal is to have the whole population participate in the group data-gathering sessions. If this is not possible, a significant sample of the population is required. The groups should also be formed cross-functionally to enable the members to view the organization from a variety of perspectives.

Individual Interviews

While it can be expensive, the individual interview is best advised when the situation warrants it. If the college representative feels that the group process is inadequate to bring to light deeper problems, individual interviews representing a cross section of the organization should also be conducted. Often the "hidden" problems remain hidden in a group setting. Insights into interpersonal and intrapersonal communication are often best gained through individual interviews. Management's perspectives are also easily gained in this manner.

Selection of Moderator

Selection of a process moderator or facilitator is critical to the interview process. The individual must have experience in managing groups. The selection can be made from within the organization or an external consultant may be used. Objectivity is the critical element. The data collected and analyzed must be free from organizational bias.

Data Gathering

Data gathering in groups can be accomplished in brainstorming sessions that normally last one hour each session. The sessions can be facilitated by either an internal or external resource. The following generally accepted rules of brainstorming may be used: everyone contributes ideas, never criticize ideas of other group members, and record ideas of members as stated without interpretation. After the brainstorming session, the data are reviewed, edited, and discussed by the group.

It is important to keep in mind that the information discussed in group or in individual interview sessions is sensitive and strict confidentiality must be maintained. Therefore, in the data-gathering process, the facilitator must make it clear to the participants that the information will be presented in a manner that does not identify individuals or specific groups. Rather, the information is a reflection of the thinking of the individuals or groups from whom the data were gathered.

Time Required to Obtain Data

Normally, the group assessment process can be accomplished in two sessions for each group of approximately ten to fifteen. The sessions are conducted one or two weeks apart. If the sessions are conducted more than two weeks apart, momentum is lost and time should be spent to review both the process and the results of the previous session.

Individual interviews can vary in length but generally should not exceed one hour and frequently can be accomplished in considerably less time. To help obtain quality data, time should be allowed for establishing ground rules, confidence, and trust.

Extent of Environmental Assessment

As the term *environmental assessment* suggests, the interest is in all aspects of an employee's work life and work environment. To conduct this type of assessment, then, data must be gathered that address both of those areas. We have found that a series of open-ended questions yields a wealth of information that we can use in the process. The types of questions include, but are not limited to, those dealing with the individuals' understanding of assigned or imposed tasks and how they perceive the importance of those tasks in the overall organizational mission, those dealing with perceived obstacles to task accomplishment, those dealing with how individuals believe that their task performance could be enhanced through organizational initiatives, and those dealing with specific training and education to enhance present skills and develop new skills.

The work life environmental assessment is more than an instrument. It is a process that customizes the assessment and gives the organization an active role in learning how to capture data that can be used for training and development. The data are then analyzed by the college representative who is facilitating the process. They are also analyzed by the organization's representatives. Together, they write up the joint evaluation that includes the cause-and-effect analysis.

When data are gathered from a wide cross section where input was encouraged, the commitment to the initiatives that are then recommended will be much greater. Initiatives may or may not call for training and instruction. Noninstructional services such as career counseling or child care may also be indicated.

Use of Information

Whatever the outcome, the use of the information is critical. Frequently, if training is indicated, the formation of an in-house team is recommended. The team then recommends action steps. Team membership should include individuals from all across the organization. The group's task is fourfold: (1) to specify training requirements and approve the training plan based on present and future assessments, (2) to communicate the training initiatives across the organization, (3) to provide ongoing evaluation of the training, and (4) to motivate participants through recognition and other incentive systems.

The facilitator or an assigned member of the group collects the data on flip charts. The data are transcribed and copies are given to each group member. Again, it is important to remember that the data are confidential and that the information must remain in the group until it has been edited, reviewed, and documented in a format previously agreed on.

Typically, the data are presented as percentages of responses to the various questions. As an example, the responses to a question dealing with obstacles to task performance may include physical plant obstacles, equipment concerns, supervisory concerns, or concerns about performance processes. The report would include the percentage of responses in each of these categories. With the approval of the group, a sample of actual responses would also be included.

Assessing Company Culture

Other processes used to assess organizational climate include various surveys that can be designed and customized to the specific environment. These instruments can measure a variety of climate issues by assessing employee perceptions on training and education, skill levels, as well as general cultural concerns such as work ethic, approaches to problem solving in the workplace, team building, and learning styles. Company culture can be assessed as broadly or cross-sectionally as the educator and the company desire. As part of a customized education plan, the culture assessment of a company yields valuable information that can inform the process of developing a successful company education plan.

Specific Assessment Tools

A culture assessment tool provides a template for gathering background information on company culture. It includes company and employee demographics, work schedule, education level and education and training involvement, job competencies, and so on. This is critical information for the design of an education process and plan in any organization. Additionally, the tool should be designed to provide the education provider with a list of tasks and responsible persons to consider as each step of the assessment process is undertaken.

The voluntary education survey is a more detailed instrument designed to measure particular environmental factors in a specific workplace, a list that is changed or customized to accommodate each environment and appropriately reflect the issues or concerns that the education provider and the company agree are critical to the development of a companywide education plan. Tabulated results are analyzed to indicate level of agreement or disagreement and, as such, constitute a self-assessment of environmental factors by employees.

Employees are asked to mark a survey tool using a continuum stating whether they strongly agree, agree, disagree, or strongly disagree with a variety of statements, all of which relate to their needs, values, perceptions, and interactions on the job. Some of the statements have to do with fellow workers and the respondents' interactions with them.

The topics of other statements may include personal education and career goals as well as personal values (for example, "I know where I want to be five years from now"). Team work and problem solving are other aspects of environmental culture that the survey can examine (for example, "Before a solution to a problem is chosen, my fellow workers discuss the pros and cons of several solutions"). Statements about individual initiative and its encouragement by the company typically are included (for example, "I have ideas about how to solve problems my fellow workers face"). The perception of autonomy can be addressed with several statements (for example, "I like to do things my own way") as can individuals' notions about work ethic (for example, "Work is satisfying to me," "The quality of work I do is meaningful to me," and "Working hard is important to me"). Values also can be examined in the tool (for example, "Honesty is something I value," "I work only for a paycheck," and "It's important for me to feel appreciated at work").

Learning styles are also included in a climate survey (for example, "I learn best by reading instructions" and "I prefer to learn new skills by watching others"). Perceived attitude of the company about education and career goals is also recorded (for example, "We have a formal process for career planning" and "The company tries to increase employee knowledge and job skills").

Summary of Results

The results of a comprehensive environmental survey should be summarized using percentages and all other accepted practices of confidentiality. The questions should be categorized by the factors measured (for example, work ethic responses). The report should contain a brief narrative that summarizes the qualified responses.

By assessing the cultural climate of an organization as a first step, education providers can gather essential baseline information about an organization and hence provide a guide for more skills-specific assessment, curriculum development, delivery, and evaluation. A work life environmental assessment is an excellent way to begin a customized training project. It affords the trainers and the company a means to determine need and a way to plan the response to that need. A customized assessment can lead to a well-designed customized training project.

JACQUES BERNIER, NANCY JACKSON, and DAVID MOORE are managers of customized training at the Community College of Aurora, Aurora, Colorado. Bernier specializes in management training, Jackson specializes in communication, and Moore is a work force literacy and education specialist.

Innovations in nontraditional customized training will continue to transform the entrepreneurial enterprise of community colleges. In the process, the training patterns of the institutions will change as well.

New Frontiers: Nontraditional Customized Training

Cary A. Israel

Yesterday, a businesswoman was negotiating an agreement with Libre, Inc., in Madrid that will allow her company to establish a market presence in Spain. It was exciting to apply the Spanish she learned in the course Doing Business in Spanish-Speaking Countries. Today, she will be in Kuwait to explore their customs before deciding whether her corporation should do business in that country. She does not want to make the mistake that a company made last year when it sent five hundred pounds of pork to several Kuwaiti restaurants. Muslims generally do not eat pork!

These events all happened by working with her local community college. Using virtual reality technology, she practiced making business decisions before they actually happened. One can be immersed in a culture and environment without every stepping foot into that society. Mistakes can occur without losing business.

This is one example of the new frontiers that lie ahead in nontraditional customized training. Multicultural customized training packages will expand beyond the frontiers of the classroom and, through technology such as virtual reality, reach into international marketplaces to provide training that will maximize opportunities for international business.

New frontiers are rarely developed by a single individual. Rather, they are often the products of vision and teamwork. And so it is with the five nontraditional customized training frontiers described in this chapter. Each requires the development of a partnership in one form or another in order to accomplish a greater good for all parties concerned, whether students, colleges, businesses, or the community at large. The first frontier or initiative examines how a consortium can better deliver customized training. The second explains how instructional design centers can maximize training quality. In the third frontier, a case is made for building a sense of community and service across generations. Modernization and transformation of business and industry through partnering with business and industry is the subject of the fourth frontier. The fifth describes the utilization and training of older workers, an important resource for business, education, and the community.

Frontier 1: Creating Consortia

In the last decade of this century it will be necessary, because of limited resources and the explosion of knowledge, for community colleges to develop more effective training systems. By using the consortium concept, a more efficient and effective approach to customized training can be provided. Consortia allow for a pooling of a variety of resources. Financial and human resources, technical expertise, and other elements combine to improve the quality and scope of the project. The activities of a consortium, if structured properly, will eliminate duplicative efforts and will lead to cost savings. While this concept requires shared decision making on items such as marketing, contracts, curricula, class size, and entrance requirements, these challenges are not insurmountable and, in fact, can result in the kind of benefits gained through teamwork and networking. Consortia should be and are being developed now within our progressive colleges. Departments are working together and boundaries are evaporating in order to improve the education of our students. Interdisciplinary curricula, team and concert teaching, and a blending of credit and customized training now occur as the norm.

Consortia should be developed outside the college as well. For example, many community colleges are delivering training to small- and medium-size businesses engaged in manufacturing. Would it not make more sense to develop a manufacturing consortium composed of community colleges, research universities, and business and industry training centers to ensure a comprehensive approach? The consortium would enable businesses to better understand and implement new manufacturing technologies and management techniques to compete in the global marketplace. It could help businesses with technology transfer and commercialization of their products. A training consortium could select the best customized training to help the employees become technically competent, develop rigorous quality tactics, and reduce or eliminate scrap.

Community colleges tend to worry about our own market penetration and who crosses our borders. We have become very territorial within our institutions and within our districts. Why? It would make more sense to compete (Latin *competere*, "to strive together for") and increase our markets rather than try to meet all the needs regardless of our competencies, capacities, and resources. We could create a stellar computer-integrated manufacturing cell without walls. Individual modules could be developed and delivered at different sites. Instead of developing a limited training manufacturing program, we could develop an extensive module that would be integrated with the other modules offered by the other organizations.

Thus, a manufacturing plant located in an urban or a rural setting could receive customized training through a regional consortium. Likewise, new and small businesses could access contemporary ideas, resources, marketing strategies, and standards and regulations. Collaborative models such as these will provide diverse training opportunities for our work force that will enable us to compete in the global marketplace.

Some of the challenges facing businesses today are whether they are capable of meeting their technology needs, developing innovative products for global markets, keeping pace with their competitors, maintaining a vibrant work force, solving manufacturing problems that affect productivity, and a myriad of other issues. Similarly, community colleges have the same type of demands. We must respond quickly to the needs of our communities, invest more heavily in acquiring appropriate educational technology, and develop and integrate new systems to ensure cost-effectiveness and quality outcomes. Accordingly, we should link up and create consortia to solve our mutual problems. We truly will become community colleges rather than colleges in a community.

Frontier 2: Instructional Design Centers for Knowledge Choreographers

The components of customized training—the learner, the learning process, and the subjects to be learned—are constantly changing. All of them affect the instructor in the teaching and learning process. To accommodate all of the changes and deliver a customized product that is high quality, state-of-the-art, and just-in-time to business, industry, and government (BIG), instructors must become *knowledge choreographers.*

Just as other types of choreographers must set the stage and orchestrate precise movements, so too instructors must orchestrate the learning process. They must make important decisions on the scope, pattern, and frequency of the information that must be conveyed from a vast quantity of knowledge. They must employ the available technology, whether interactive video systems, telecommunications, computer-aided instruction, virtual reality, or a mixture thereof. It is, indeed, a challenging but rewarding undertaking.

Customized trainers should establish *instructional design centers* to foster effective training and educate these new knowledge choreographers. These teaching-learning-research centers should be available to BIG on a contract basis. These centers should be able to respond rapidly to the design, development, and implementation of programs to accommodate BIG needs.

The problem for some institutions is that they lack the expertise and resources needed to deliver state-of-the-art education choreographed to the customers' needs on a regular, or even occasional, basis. The formation of regional instructional design centers would enable them to deliver customized education in a timely state-of-the-art fashion without the large investment. Such centers could not only foster effective training for BIG but also be available to assist credit programs as well as customized training programs of colleges that participate.

Colleges that develop as instructional design centers could provide assistance through technological link-up or on-site consultation to fellow colleges as well as to their own students and faculty (and BIG). The teaching-learning process would constantly be researched and developed, including all of those components of customized (and credit) education that are constantly changing: the learner, the learning process (including all available technology), and the subjects to be learned. Knowledge choreographers would only be strengthened by orchestrating their work with instructional design centers.

One may argue that our resources are limited and that we should not establish such centers. But it may be detrimental if we do not! Massive restructuring is occurring throughout our society. We must be ready, able, and prepared if we are to improve our accountability. Resource reallocation and prioritization of mission will allow the thoughtful development of the teaching-learning-research centers. These centers not only should be available to BIG but should also be adequately staffed to accommodate the credit programs at the colleges. The community benefits, the colleges benefit, and, more important, the employee or student profits.

Frontier 3: Intergenerational Service Learning Programs

In *Building Communities: A Vision for a New Century*, the Commission on the Future of Community Colleges (1988) called for action to strengthen our communities. We must commence with the building of communities but also we must realize that intergenerational service programs will allow us to recapture the spirit of community. Intergenerational programs are defined as activities that bring old and young together for their mutual benefit (Angelis, 1990). "Hundreds, perhaps thousands, of intergenerational programs have been initiated, including child and adult day care centers, elementary and secondary schools, youth shelters, colleges and universities, senior centers, senior residences, hospitals, nursing homes, and foster care homes" (Ventura-Markel, Liederman, and Ossofsky, 1989, p. 174).

However, we are just beginning to understand and develop programs designed to strengthen the connections across generations that once existed forty or fifty years ago. As our country's infrastructure has crumbled over the last thirty years, and generations have stopped living in close proximity, it seems as if our communities also have deteriorated. Yet, we continue to adhere to past conventional wisdom.

For instance, when we enter a record store at our local mall, it is interesting to see that there are no records in the record store. We find compact disks and tapes but no records. Why do we still refer to them as record stores? Similarly, we can observe that senior centers, senior residences, hospitals, and grocery stores are not located on community college campuses. Why not? Maybe because of antiquated zoning laws or because that is how we have envisioned our colleges. We develop wonderful learning communities but we leave out the intergenerational concept. In fact, we must usually import the seniors to our campuses.

Customized trainers can help forge new ground by formulating new programs that address our social problems and that develop safety nets for our citizens. We have been reluctant to enter into such social programs because of limited funds and our adherence to our traditional mission. Our diffidence must come to an end. The 1990s will see a resurgence of community services and initiatives to strengthen families, communities, and our educational systems. The process has already begun, and it will proceed with lightning speed.

Our community colleges should be at the forefront of this movement. We should create intergenerational campuses, and we should come together to develop community strategies. Our institutional plans should meet community needs and reflect the values, traditions, and diversity of the surrounding areas. By coming together, we can provide critical information about employment, AIDS, child care, elder care, nutrition and wellness, and much more. Again, our approach is often too fragmented. For example, we use the Senior Corps of Retired Executives to help develop business plans for our new small businesses. Do we ever survey these volunteers to obtain information about their other interests in relation to college endeavors? Are we making optimum use of the talents of retired faculty by creating a corps of faculty emeriti or utilizing retired groundskeepers to show us efficient conservation methods? Probably not, but we should begin.

In future campus master plans, we may want the community services and customized training department to help build a "true" community college campus. The campus could include residential apartments where seniors and students reside, where day-care centers thrive because of senior volunteers, where senior mentors can prepare us for future challenges, where retired faculty can help establish effective teaching strategies, and where we all can roam and enjoy our surroundings after attending a multitude of cultural events.

Frontier 4: Quality and Modernization of the United States

Technology development and new business strategies have altered how we conduct business and interact with our customers. American business needs to incorporate Total Quality Management (TQM) and ISO 9000 standards, and to modernize and convert to high-quality performance environments.

TQM is being incorporated into management systems around the globe.

TQM focuses on change as a natural part of the organizational system. Additionally, TQM provides for increased employee visibility and authority and better performance accountability. Our colleges are being asked regularly to provide TQM training for BIG. The demands will increase while we go through this major restructuring or technological evolution.

The quality movement compelled the International Organization for Standardization (ISO is the European abbreviation) to create ISO 9000, which is a series of standards that a company can use to set up a quality management system. The object of ISO 9000 is to promote the development of standardization with a view toward facilitating international exchange of goods and services and developing cooperation in intellectual, scientific, technological, and economic activities. The standards are generic, not specific to any particular product or service industry, and can be used by manufacturing and service companies alike. These standards were developed to maintain an efficient and competitive quality system for business.

The ISO 9000 series consists of five separate quality system models: ISO 9000, 9001, 9002, 9003, and 9004, from which companies select the model or models that apply to their products or services. It is an integrated system linking various company processes into one system. For example, a quality program may call for the use of statistical process control techniques in manufacturing, quality cost accounting in operations, and design reviews in engineering. ISO 9000 combines all these different programs into one overall standard system. There are well-documented reasons to implement an ISO 9000 system, such as internal improvement, market positioning, supplier control, and customer or regulatory requirements.

An increasing number of companies and organizations are becoming involved in today's global economy, and ISO regulations are going to affect them. The list of products affected continues to grow and includes items such as toys, simple pressure vessels, implantable medical devices, construction products, machinery, and telecommunications equipment.

Under the banner of modernization and conversion, there is a fully collaborative governmentwide effort called the Technology Reinvestment Project. This initiative seeks to stimulate the transition to a growing, integrated, national industrial capability to provide the most advanced, affordable military systems and the most competitive commercial products. It also intends to create jobs in the long term by converting defense manufacturing systems to commercial product development. Community colleges will be participating in the area of manufacturing education and training. We will help design "teaching factories" and we should integrate apprenticeship and technology-preparation models into this concept. Under this broad category, we will retrain the manufacturing work force, develop manufacturing education coalitions, and establish manufacturing technology and outreach centers. Focus areas will be health care technology, training and instructional technology, vehicle and aeronautical technologies, materials and structures manufacturing, mechanical and electronics design and manufacturing, and information infrastructure. The opportunities are ripe for customized training in the entire field of modernization and conversion.

Frontier 5: Utilizing Older Workers

The principles and philosophies surrounding education and training for our community college students are especially important to older workers. Advances in technology, workplace modernization, and the accompanying demands for a highly skilled work force make the training of older workers a vital part of the community college mission. The 1989 Louis Harris survey found that 37 percent of people between the ages of fifty and sixty-four who were currently employed wanted to continue to work past the normal time of retirement if their employers would train them for new positions. The survey also found that 29 percent of people age fifty to sixty-four who were retired would have accepted retraining by their last employers in order to continue working (Harris Poll, 1989).

Older workers have not lost their ability to perform; they are simply in danger of becoming victims of a rapidly changing global economy and the ripples of that new economy on job skills. The U.S. Department of Labor estimates that by the year 2000 a worker will change careers three times and change jobs at least seven times. There will be an urgent need to retrain workers as they move from one job to another (Commission on the Future of Community Colleges, 1988). We have all realized that lifelong learning is a necessity and that eventually everyone becomes an older worker. It is not in our best interest to waste the talent and expertise of this important sector.

According to the U.S. Census Bureau, among available workers the percentage who are twenty-five to thirty-four years of age is projected to drop from 19 percent to 16 percent in the year 2000, and the proportion of available workers age forty-five to fifty-four will increase from 10 percent to 16 percent (U.S. Bureau of the Census, 1983). Thus, older worker retraining is an important new direction for higher education, for our nation, and for the countless number of older workers who want to maintain their productivity and their contributions.

Conclusion

There will be ample opportunities for customized training activities in the future. We should not be timid about redesigning the entire academy. Are we not, in fact, pursuing that entrepreneurial spirit on our campuses? Too often, those involved agonize about their roles at the college. The health of community colleges in the future will be determined by how well all of us collaborate and exchange ideas. Our communities will be reborn only if we take bold steps to change patterns that no longer work.

As we approach the last decade of this century and move into the second millennium, it is incumbent that we remember the past. History does indeed repeat itself. In the period 993–998 before the first millennium, there were famines and wars throughout the world, religion had lost its efficacy, educational systems were under attack, lawlessness and corruption abounded, and there was a widening gap between the nobility and the poor. This time period was known as the "years of darkness and despair." It was a common belief that the world would come to an end in the year 999.

In 1993, we too have famines and wars, our educational systems are under attack, poverty is increasing as is unemployment, and there is a widening gap between rich and poor. The world, of course, did not end in the year 999, and in fact a period after 1000 was known as the "hopeful years." We make history, and all of us must ensure that customized training permits all of us to have hopeful years as we proceed toward the year 2000 and beyond.

References

Angelis, J. "Bringing Old and Young Together." *Vocational Education Journal,* 1990, *65,* 19–21.

Commission on the Future of Community Colleges. *Building Communities: A Vision for a New Century.* Washington, D.C.:American Association of Community and Junior Colleges, 1988. 58pp. (ED 293 578)

Harris Poll. New York: Louis Harris and Associates, Inc., 1989.

U.S. Department of Commerce. Bureau of the Census. *Census of Population.* Washington, D.C.: U.S. Government Printing Office, 1983.

Ventura-Markel, C., Liederman, D. S., and Ossofsky, J. "Exemplary Intergenerational Programs." In S. Newman (ed.), *Intergenerational Programs.* 1989.

CARY A. ISRAEL *is executive director of the Illinois Community College Board, the third largest community college system in the nation. The system is composed of forty-nine community colleges enrolling nearly one million students annually.*

This annotated bibliography lists ERIC documents on customized contract training, including an overview with analyses of one national survey and one Colorado statewide survey, and provides a section on planning, promoting, managing, and evaluating customized education programs and a section on building partnerships between colleges and their communities.

Sources and Information: Customized Training in the Community Colleges

David Deckelbaum

This volume explores the customized contract training being offered by two-year institutions of higher education. Emphasis is placed on continual assessment of the needs of business, industry, labor, and government entities so that meaningful partnerships can be formed to ensure that programs meet current workplace demands and also to plan for future economic requirements.

The following citations reflect the current ERIC literature on customized contract training in the community college. Most ERIC documents can be viewed on microfiche at approximately nine hundred libraries worldwide. In addition, most can be ordered on microfiche or in paper copy from the ERIC Document Reproduction Service at (800) 443-ERIC.

An Overview of Customized Contract Education and Analyses of a National Survey and a Statewide Survey

Several surveys examine the status and practices of community college involvement in economic activities and labor force development through relationships with external organizations.

Kantor, S. L. *Direct Services to Businesses Delivered by Colorado Community Colleges.* Denver: Colorado Community College and Occupational Education System, 1991. 43 pp. (ED 343 633)

A statewide survey was conducted to document and analyze the variety of direct services to businesses and industry provided by Colorado's fifteen community colleges. At each college, the president and the individual responsible for direct instructional services to business participated in both a survey questionnaire and a personal interview. The findings, based on returns from fourteen colleges, include the following: (1) Colorado community colleges customized their direct services to business over 50 percent of the time, compared to national figures indicating that over 50 percent of business services by community colleges were modified or off-the-shelf versions of regular course offerings; (2) 50.6 percent of the courses offered focused on job-specific vocational skills; (3) the highest volume of instructional services was concentrated in eight colleges where economic conditions were strong and the population sizes were large, whereas noninstructional services were spread evenly among the community colleges around the state; (4) more employers purchased noninstructional services, such as customized small business services, than instructional services; and (5) state economic initiatives accounted for 17 percent of the employees receiving customized training. The study report includes a list of recommendations, reflections on the future missions of community colleges, and statistical data on study findings.

Lynch, R., Palmer, J. C., and Grubb, W. N. *Community College Involvement in Contract Training and Other Economic Development Activities.* Washington, D.C.: American Association of Community and Junior Colleges; Berkeley: National Center for Research in Vocational Education, University of California, Berkeley, 1991. 66 pp. (ED 339 434) (Available from the National Center for Research in Vocational Education Materials Distribution Service, Western Illinois University, 46 Horrabin Hall, Macomb, IL 61455.)

In 1989–1990, a national survey was conducted to assess the scope and nature of contract training and other economic development activities at community colleges and technical institutes. The survey was sent to a random sample of 246 community colleges, requesting information on the colleges' work force and economic development activities in 1988–1989. Major findings, based on a 72 percent response rate, include the following: (1) The majority (94 percent) of the public community colleges in the sample offered at least one course on a contract basis to public or private employers; (2) most colleges had relatively modest contract education programs, with 50 as the median number of courses offered, 919 as the median number of students enrolled, and 24 as the median number of employer clients served; (3) frequently offered contract courses dealt with job-specific skills, basic reading, writing, and mathematics skills, and miscellaneous courses; (4) on average, private firms comprised approximately 70 percent of the employer clients served by community college contract education programs; (5) on average, 61 percent of job-specific courses offered were developed jointly by the colleges and their clients; (6) employers provided the largest share of revenues needed to support contract education, followed by subsidies from state and local governments; and (7) approximately 80 percent of the public community, technical, and junior colleges received funds through the Vocational Education Act, approximately 50 percent received Job Training Partnership Act funds, and approximately 50 percent received funds from other state, local, and federal agencies that support business assistance programs or vocational training. Data tables and the survey instrument are included.

Planning, Promoting, Managing, and Evaluating Customized Education

A successful program devoted to providing customized training services requires up-to-date information on local economic needs as well as national and global trends. Services must be developed, promoted, and evaluated on their ability to meet client needs as well as on the extent to which they reflect institutional objectives, goals, and missions.

Bragg, D. D., and Jacobs, J. *A Conceptual Framework for Evaluating Community College Customized Training Programs*. Berkeley: National Center for Research in Vocational Education, University of California, Berkeley, 1991. 50 pp. (ED 338 866) (Available from the National Center for Research in Vocational Education Materials Distribution Service, Western Illinois University, 46 Horrabin Hall, Macomb, IL 61455 [order no. MDS-175].)

This project developed an operational definition of and designed a conceptual framework for evaluating customized training programs offered by two-year postsecondary education institutions. The definition specifies that customized training requires the following: contracts, payments, relationships to economic development strategies, delivery of training designed to improve work force competencies, and adaptation to the needs of external clients. Four categories further differentiate training approaches: custom-designed courses, modification of courses, alternative delivery of courses, and courses for special populations. The framework contains sets of variables that describe the context for customized training. The variables reflect characteristics of employees and employers, institutions, communities, and states that affect how customized training is conducted. The process identifies the client needs and proceeds through the subprocesses of negotiation, job analysis, instructional design, implementation, program evaluation, and administration.

Deegan, W. L. *Managing Contract Training Programs: Progress and Proposals*. Institute for Studies in Higher Education Policy Paper No. 2. Tallahassee: Institute for Studies in Higher Education, Florida State University, 1988. 27 pp. (ED 294 616)

An overview is provided of community college involvement in job training for industry on a contract basis. Part One provides background on the changing role of community colleges and the introduction of contract training as a means of·addressing the growing need of organizations to train and retrain staff. Part Two offers a national perspective on the boom in training and development, indicating that only 57 percent of all employee training programs are provided in-house and listing the types of education and nonschool organizations offering the other 43 percent of employee training. This section also considers statewide efforts to address economic development needs. Part Three presents a national profile of contract training in community colleges, using survey data to examine the organizational structures needed to deliver contract training, trends related to program sites and the college-credit status of courses, types of contract clients, problems, benefits, and perceptions of the future of contract training. Part Four discusses issues in the management of contract training programs, including program organization, planning, finance, and evaluation. Finally, Part Five identifies policy issues related to the establishment of separate business institutes, the goals and limits of a center for contract training, separate advisory structures for representatives from business and the college, staffing needs, and financial policies.

Shubird, E. *Developing Short-Term Training Programs.* Montgomery: Alabama State Department of Education, Division of Vocational Education Services, 1990. 31 pp. (ED 331 976)

This manual offers guidelines for vocational educators who want to develop and conduct short-term training programs for business and industry. The guide is organized into six chapters. Chapter One reviews opportunities in short-term training, discusses commonly applied principles of competency-based training, and suggests a practical model for developing short-term training. The next five chapters are based on the five steps of the model: determining training needs, specifying training objectives, developing a performance evaluation system, developing the training plan, and developing performance guides. Examples and checklists are provided throughout the chapters. Two appendices offer a performance guide for short-term training development and a four-part outline for conducting short-term interactive training.

Creating Partnerships with the Community, Business, Industry, Government, and Labor Organizations

Collaboration between custom training service providers and their clients, from the planning stages through program evaluation, is essential in order to maintain course relevance and quality.

Grubb, W. N. *The Developing Vocational Education and Training "System": Partnerships and Customized Training.* Reprint series. Berkeley: National Center for Research in Vocational Education, University of California, Berkeley, 1989. 24 pp. (ED 329 680) (Available from the National Center for Research in Vocational Education Materials Distribution Service, 46 Horrabin Hall, Western Illinois University, Macomb, IL 61455 [order no. MDS-230].)

One legacy of the United States' emphasis on individualism is a system of vocational education disconnected from employers. Collaboration is an attempt to replace hostility with closer relations between the public and private sectors. The movement for partnerships comes as the "system" of work-related education and training is becoming increasingly complex due to institutional expansion, dissatisfaction with components of the system, and the discovery of new needs. Customized training is one particular kind of partnership between employers and public education and training institutions. Advantages to vocational institutions include the connection with employers, vocational programs kept current by firms' contributions of equipment, new opportunities for combining general and specific training, and a placement mechanism. Drawbacks to customized training include shifts in employment, potential bias in the composition of trainees, and narrow vocationalism. An analysis of some customized training programs shows that many programs have the potential for exploiting their strengths. The implications are that customized training should be more systematically evaluated, states and the federal government should ensure that economic development efforts do not merely reallocate existing employment, and vocational education should be targeted to businesses that might expand employment and production.

Hines, T. E. "Creative Alliances with the Business Community: Pima Community College." Paper presented at the annual international conference on leadership development of the League for Innovation in the Community College, "Leadership 2000," San Francisco, July 1990. 16 pp. (ED 322 958)

Pima Community College (PCC) in Tucson is involved in a number of creative alliances with the Arizona business community, including the Arizona Consortium for Education and Training and the Arizona State Environmental Technical Training Center (ASETT). Through the Consortium for Education, PCC, in conjunction with Arizona's four-year colleges, provides specific technical training required by participating businesses and firms in the area. Monthly meetings between member businesses and colleges are devoted to discussing new, ongoing, and needed programs and services. The consortium is effective because it is informal, open to any organization, and places limited demands on members. ASETT is one of approximately forty regional centers sponsored by the U.S. Environmental Protection Agency. The academic component of the program focuses on water treatment and distribution, wastewater treatment and collection, and hazardous materials and solid waste. Students can earn one-year advanced certificates or an associate's degree in applied science. ASETT provides the business community with statewide technical seminars and contract training. Enrollments in the academic program have grown by more than 128 percent over the past three years. The success of these college-business programs is attributable to the fact the PCC is doing what community colleges do well—teaching, curriculum, and related educational areas. An attachment provides brief outlines of these and other programs linking PCC with the business community and includes the names of contact persons.

Phelps, L. A., Brandenburg, D. C., and Jacobs, J. *The UAW Joint Funds: Opportunities and Dilemmas for Postsecondary Vocational Education.* Berkeley: National Center for Research in Vocational Education, University of California, Berkeley, 1990. 45 pp. (ED 328 765) (Available from the National Center for Research in Vocational Education Materials Distribution Service, 46 Horrabin Hall, Western Illinois University, Macomb, IL 61455 [order no. MDS-119].)

This study examined the impact that the United Auto Workers (UAW) Joint Funds programs, established in the early 1980s, have had on the policies and practices of select community colleges in the Midwest. Each of the three UAW Joint Funds programs (Ford, General Motors, and Chrysler) offers a wide array of special programs to active and inactive workers. Study data were collected through interviews with college presidents and program representatives, site visits, and reviews of case studies. Information was received from eight community colleges in Illinois and Michigan that had worked closely with the UAW Joint Funds programs for the prior three years. The study found that the UAW Joint Funds programs have extended a new model for industrial relations that emphasizes concern for human resources development. The existence of the joint funds has enhanced the direct involvement of the community colleges in providing customized training programs and courses. The varied programs provided in the plants also directly reflected and supported the broad mission of the community colleges. However, the colleges' broader view of educational planning operated in only a limited way in the programs. The short-term needs or timetables of the programs sometimes conflicted with the community colleges' ability to respond. Little research exists with which to evaluate the programs. Recommendations were made for improving the accountability of the programs.

DAVID DECKELBAUM is user services coordinator at the ERIC Clearinghouse for Community Colleges, University of California, Los Angeles.

INDEX

Ordering Information

NEW DIRECTIONS FOR COMMUNITY COLLEGES is a series of paperback books that provides expert assistance to help community colleges meet the challenges of their distinctive and expanding educational mission. Books in the series are published quarterly in Spring, Summer, Fall, and Winter and are available for purchase by subscription and individually.

SUBSCRIPTIONS for 1994 cost $49.00 for individuals (a savings of 25 percent over single-copy prices) and $72.00 for institutions, agencies, and libraries. Please do not send institutional checks for personal subscriptions. Standing orders are accepted.

SINGLE COPIES cost $16.95 when payment accompanies order. (California, New Jersey, New York, and Washington, D.C., residents please include appropriate sales tax.) Billed orders will be charged postage and handling.

DISCOUNTS FOR QUANTITY ORDERS are available. Please write to the address below for information.

ALL ORDERS must include either the name of an individual or an official purchase order number. Please submit your order as follows:
  Subscriptions: specify series and year subscription is to begin
  Single copies: include individual title code (such as CC82)

MAIL ALL ORDERS TO:
  Jossey-Bass Publishers
  350 Sansome Street
  San Francisco, California 94104-1342

FOR SINGLE-COPY SALES OUTSIDE OF THE UNITED STATES, CONTACT:
  Maxwell Macmillan International Publishing Group
  866 Third Avenue
  New York, New York 10022-6221

FOR SUBSCRIPTION SALES OUTSIDE OF THE UNITED STATES, contact any international subscription agency or Jossey-Bass directly.

OTHER TITLES AVAILABLE IN THE
NEW DIRECTIONS FOR COMMUNITY COLLEGES SERIES
Arthur M. Cohen, Editor-in-Chief
Florence B. Brawer, Associate Editor